DISCOVER DINOSAURS

Become a Dinosaur Detective

by Dr. Chris McGowan

illustrations by Tina Holdcroft

A ROYAL ONTARIO MUSEUM BOOK

Addison-Wesley Publishing Company

Reading, Massachusetts   Menlo Park, California   New York
Don Mills, Ontario   Wokingham, England   Amsterdam   Bonn
Sydney   Singapore   Tokyo   Madrid   San Juan
Paris   Seoul   Milan   Mexico City   Taipei

To A FATHER WHO ENCOURAGED HIS SON.

Written by Christopher McGowan for the Royal Ontario Museum.

Library of Congress Cataloging-in-Publication Data

McGowan, Christopher.
    Discover dinosaurs : become a dinosaur detective / by Chris
McGowan ; illustrations by Tina Holdcroft.
        p.   cm.
    "A Royal Ontario Museum book."
    Includes index.
    Summary: Uses hands-on activities to present information about
dinosaurs and to show how paleontologists have learned about these
prehistoric creatures.
    ISBN 0-201-62267-X
    1. Dinosaurs—Juvenile literature. [1. Dinosaurs.   2. Fossils.
3. Paleontology—Experiments.   4. Experiments.   5. Scientific
recreations.]   I. Holdcroft, Tina, ill.   II. Title.
QE862.D5M26 1993
567.9′1—dc20   92-42627
                                                           CIP
                                                           AC

Note: the word "deduction" is used in this book in the everyday sense of
"reasoning," not in the strict sense of reasoning from the general to the
particular.

Originally published by   Edited by Valerie Wyatt
Kids Can Press Ltd.,   Book design by N.R. Jackson
Toronto, Ontario.   Typeset by Compeer
                                      Typographic Services Limited
1 2 3 4 5 6 7 8 9–96959493   Printed and bound in Canada
First printing, February 1993

Text stock contains over 50% recycled paper

Acknowledgments

Writing for children was a challenge that was made considerably easier for me by the expert editorial help I received from Valerie Wyatt. I thank her for her patient help and for this valuable learning experience. I also wish to thank Elizabeth MacLeod for the meticulous care with which she steered the final manuscript through its numerous final stages. Tina Holdcroft transformed my written words into fun illustrations with great skill and imagination, for which I thank her. Thanks also to Ricky Englander and Valerie Hussey of Kids Can Press, Hugh Porter of Publication Services at the Royal Ontario Museum, and Catherine Hollett. As well, I am very grateful to Dr. Andrew Forester who read the entire manuscript and made many helpful suggestions. Liz McGowan read early drafts of the manuscript and gave valuable advice, criticism and encouragement—as always.

Contents

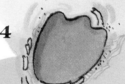

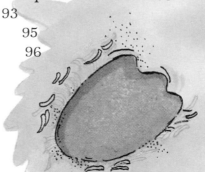

Dinosaur detective

Just imagine if you could step into a time machine and travel back to the age of dinosaurs. Pick a time—100 million years ago will do. Ready . . . here we go!

It's going to be a warm day. The sun has already driven the mist off the lake and has climbed well clear of the treetops. Take a deep breath—there's a fresh scent of pine in the air.

What's that over there? Look, in the clearing in front of the trees—there's a whole herd of them! They're huge, the size of elephants. What on earth are they? This is our first encounter with dinosaurs. We have come upon a herd of iguanodons. Fortunately, they aren't dangerous. Some of them walk slowly down to the water's edge to drink, but most of them are more interested in chewing on the plants that grow in the clearing.

Suddenly the dinosaurs closest to the trees stop feeding and rise up onto their hind legs to look around. Something must have startled them. Now they're all standing and looking. They're very nervous—and so are we! The next moment, panic breaks out in the herd. Dinosaurs dash off in all directions. Although they walk on all fours, they run on their hind legs. Now we can see what they were running away from—a hunting pack of dromaeosaurs. These small, fierce dinosaurs—shorter than a man—dart after the iguanodons on their hind legs.

One of the iguanodons has been surrounded. Although the dromaeosaurs are much smaller, they have some deadly weapons: a huge hooked claw on each foot. It's very sharp—so are their teeth and the claws on their fingers. And look at those powerful hind legs and stiff tails.

The dromaeosaurs hiss angrily at the cornered *Iguanodon*. One dromaeosaur steps closer. Using its tail for balance, it stands on one foot and raises the other foot high in the air. The deadly claw flashes downwards, inflicting the first wound. The other dromaeosaurs join in and soon it's all over for *Iguanodon*.

The same scene 100 million years later: the lake has long since disappeared; so have all the dinosaurs.

Instead of lush vegetation, we are tramping over sun-parched rocks. The only evidence that dinosaurs were ever here is trapped in the rocks under our feet. If we're lucky, we may find some of these bony remains in the rock. These remains are called fossils, and people who collect and study fossils are called palaeontologists.

How do palaeontologists reconstruct scenes of the remote past just by studying a lot of old bones? They look for more clues, by making comparisons with modern animals.

7

Compare the two skulls on this page. The one on the right is a modern lion; the other is a dinosaur called *Tyrannosaurus*. Notice the lion's sharp teeth. They're good for eating meat. *Tyrannosaurus* also has sharp teeth. What do you think it fed on? If you guessed meat, you'd be absolutely right. By making comparisons like this between long-dead dinosaurs and modern animals, we get clues to life in the distant past.

Palaeontologists are a bit like the detectives you see on television. They hunt for clues that the dinosaurs have left behind, then piece together a picture of how dinosaurs lived and what they looked like. But unlike TV detectives, palaeontologists don't solve crimes that happened a few days or weeks ago. They solve mysteries that happened millions of years ago.

ACTIVITY
Would you make a good dinosaur detective?

Good palaeontologists, like good detectives, must be observant and make sensible deductions from clues. How observant are you? How good are you at making deductions? Test yourself and see. Check your score on page 96.

1. Think about a room in your home, not the one you're in right now. Score one point for each correct answer.

    What colour are the drapes?

    How many chairs are there?

    Are there any windows open?

    Is there a carpet on the floor?

The famous detective Sherlock Holmes was a master of deduction (figuring things out from clues). Palaeontologists must do the same thing. How good are you at making deductions? Score one point for each correct deduction.

2. Think of someone in your family whom you've seen in the last little while but who is not in the same room as you are. Make a list of what the person is wearing. Score one point for every correct piece of clothing.

3. From the sounds (perhaps smells, too) coming from one of the rooms in your home, deduce what might be going on there.

4. Look out the window. From the way people are behaving and what they are wearing, deduce what the weather is like.

    Is the wind blowing?

    From which direction?

5. Choose a family member who is out of sight. From your knowledge of this person's habits, deduce what he or she might be doing at this very moment.

9

1. Roadside clue: discovery of the first dinosaur

Gideon Mantell was a country doctor who lived in southern England in the early 1800s. He was very interested in collecting fossils and even used part of his house for a museum. His wife, Mary Ann, used to spend a lot of time waiting with the horse and carriage while her husband paid house calls on his patients. One day, so the story goes, Mrs. Mantell picked up a small object by the roadside. When she showed it to her husband, he recognized that it was a fossil tooth. Dr. Mantell had never seen another tooth like this one. He did some detective work to find out where it had come from. The fossil was part of a load of gravel that had been used to surface the road. Dr. Mantell traced the gravel back to a quarry near the small village of Cuck-

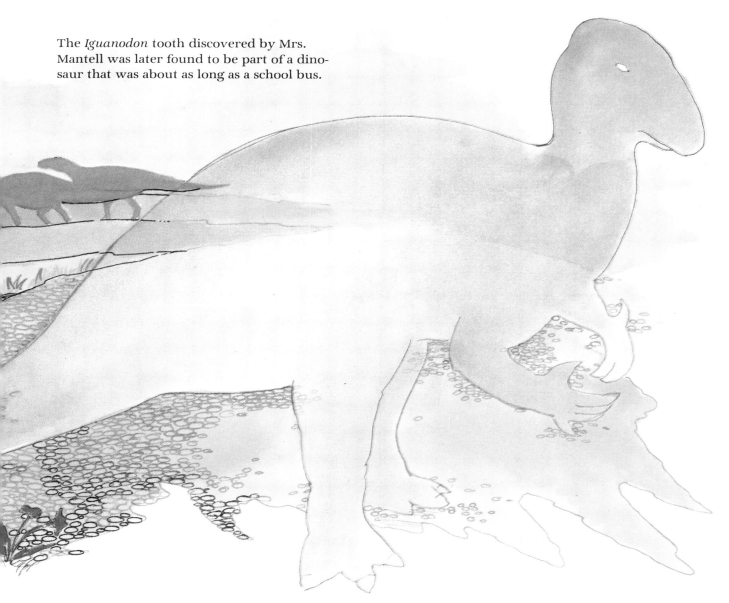

The *Iguanodon* tooth discovered by Mrs. Mantell was later found to be part of a dinosaur that was about as long as a school bus.

field, in Sussex. By patiently searching the rocks of the quarry, he found more fossil teeth and some pieces of a skeleton.

Dr. Mantell compared the fossil teeth with the teeth of living animals and concluded that the teeth belonged to some sort of reptile. The teeth looked like those of an iguana lizard, so he named the new fossil *Iguanodon*, meaning "iguana tooth."

At about the same time, a former clergyman named William Buckland found the bones of another huge reptile. This one turned out to be a meat eater and was given the name *Megalosaurus*, meaning "giant lizard." *Megalosaurus* shares a place of honour with the plant-eating *Iguanodon* as the first dinosaurs to be discovered and named. But back then, people didn't call the giant reptiles dinosaurs.

It was palaeontologist Richard Owen who came up with the name "dinosaur," meaning "terrible lizard." Owen recognized that these giant reptiles were quite different from any living reptiles. For one thing, their legs were not sprawled out at the sides like a lizard's, but were set vertically beneath the body, like our own.

How did scientists know that dinosaurs were reptiles? What are reptiles, anyway? If you said snakes and lizards are reptiles, you would be right. You might also have said crocodiles and tortoises (land turtles). Some reptiles, such as alligators and turtles and sea snakes, live in the water, but most reptiles live on dry land. Reptiles share some common features. Most have a dry scaly skin, with no hair or fur to help keep them warm. So they usually feel cold to the touch, which is why they are often called "cold-blooded." Almost all reptiles lay eggs, but theirs are different from birds' eggs because they have soft shells—they're like ping-pong balls.

Reptiles also have a backbone. Scientists call this a vertebral column, and they call animals that have them vertebrates. Are you a vertebrate? Feel down the centre of your back. Can you feel your vertebral column? Yes, you are a vertebrate. So are other mammals. In fact, there are five main types of vertebrates: fish, amphibians, reptiles (including dinosaurs), birds and mammals (including us). They differ from each other in many ways, including features of their skeletons. It is because dinosaurs have reptilian features in their skeletons that they were recognized as being reptiles.

A who's who of vertebrates

We are **mammals** and share a number of common features with other mammals such as rabbits, cats, horses, bats and cows. Mammals have hair or fur, which helps to keep their bodies warm, so they are often called "warm-blooded." Mammals also feed milk to their young, and almost every young mammal develops inside its mother's body until it is ready to be born.

Birds are familiar to all of us and are easily distinguished from other vertebrates because they have feathers to keep their bodies warm. They also have wings, most of them fly, and they all lay eggs that have hard shells.

You already know the features **reptiles** share: they have dry, scaly skin, with no fur or feathers to keep them warm, so they are often called "cold-blooded." They lay soft-shelled eggs.

Amphibians usually live in the water or in damp places. Most of them, such as frogs and newts, have wet skin that feels slimy and cold. Like reptiles, they lay eggs, but their eggs don't have a shell and are therefore usually laid in water to prevent the contents from drying out.

Fish spend all their lives in water. Like amphibians, they have a wet, slippery skin, and they are mostly cold-blooded. They have fins instead of legs and look so different from other vertebrates that we have no trouble in identifying them.

Spot the imposters

Dinosaurs were land animals. Some dinosaurs may have spent some of their time in water (just as elephants do today), but they probably didn't live in the water all of the time. As far as we know, dinosaurs didn't have fur or feathers. And remember the feature that impressed Professor Owen—their legs were not sprawled out at the sides like a lizard's, but were held under the body, like ours.

Now that you know what a dinosaur is, can you spot the dinosaur imposters shown here? Answers on page 96.

Hip dinosaurs

So far, palaeontologists have dug up and identified hundreds of different species of dinosaurs. These dinosaurs can be divided into two main groups, based on the shape of their hips, or pelvis. The bird-hipped dinosaurs, called ornithischians, have a four-pronged pelvis. The lizard-hipped dinosaurs, called saurischians, have a three-pronged pelvis.

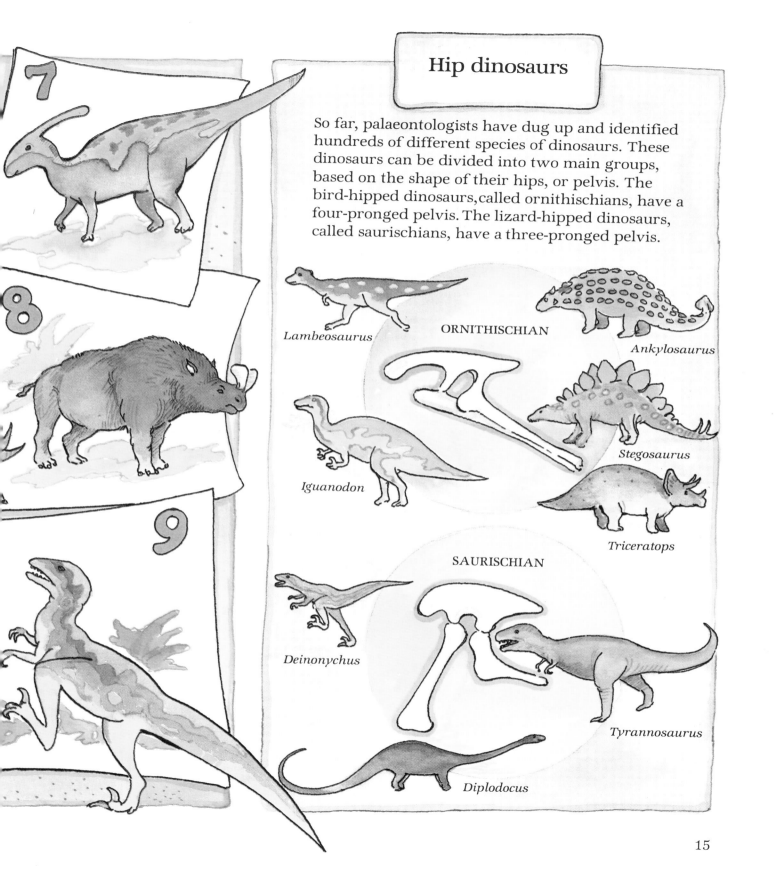

Lambeosaurus

ORNITHISCHIAN

Ankylosaurus

Iguanodon

Stegosaurus

Triceratops

SAURISCHIAN

Deinonychus

Tyrannosaurus

Diplodocus

WHEN DID DINOSAURS LIVE?

Dinosaurs first appeared on the Earth during the middle of the Triassic Period, about 240 million years ago. They survived right up to the end of the Cretaceous Period, about 65 million years ago. Why do scientists use words like Triassic and Cretaceous instead of just talking in numbers of years? The short answer is that it is a lot more convenient. The Earth is very old, about four-and-a-half billion years—that is, 4 500 000 000 years. That's a pretty large number. You'd get almost as large a number if you worked out your age in seconds. Suppose you are 10 years old, which is 10 × 365 days, or 10 × 365 × 24 × 60 × 60 seconds. Work that out with a calculator and you'll find you're a grand total of 315 360 000 seconds old. If palaeontologists always referred to the ages of their fossils in years, it would be like referring to your age in seconds. Just imagine telling one of your friends that you got your first two-wheeled bike when you were 189 216 000 seconds old! It's much easier to say that you got your bike for your sixth birthday.

Scientists carefully chose the names for the different ages. It all started over 200 years ago when people began noticing different patterns of rocks in cliffs and quarries across the land. They saw that different rock layers contained different sorts of fossils.

For example, the chalk layer is crammed full of the skeletons of microscopic animals that once lived in the sea. The chalk layer was named the Cretaceous Period because the Latin word for chalk is "creta." Fossil reptiles, including dinosaurs, are sometimes found in the chalk. Dinosaurs also occur in rock layers below the chalk, but never in layers far above the chalk. Fossil mammals, in contrast, are more often found above the chalk layer than below it. Periods are parts of Eras. The Cretaceous Period is the third and last period of the Mesozoic Era. The Mesozoic Era is often called the Age of Reptiles because reptiles were the dominant vertebrates of the time.

MESOZOIC

Triassic

Edaphosaurus   *Coelophysis*   *Ichthyosaurus*   *Dorygnathus*

16

ACTIVITY
A personal time scale

Here's your chance to invent your own "geological" time scale, complete with your own made-up names for the different time periods.

You'll need:
- scissors
- writing paper
- a pencil or a pen
- an old newspaper
- a roll of toilet paper
- tape
- a marker

Warning: markers must be used in a well-ventilated room.

1. Cut the writing paper into rectangles 4 × 2.5 cm (1½ × 1 inch). Number each piece, in years, starting from one year to your age now.

2. Spread the newspaper on the floor (to protect it when you use the marker). Unroll the toilet paper on the newspaper in a straight line.

3. For this chart, three toilet paper sheets equal one year. Tape the "one year" label at the end of the first three sheets.

4. Tape your "two year" label at the end of the next three sheets, and so on until you reach your present age.

5. Make a list of important times in your life. You might include when you started talking, began school, learned to ride a bike . . . there are lots.

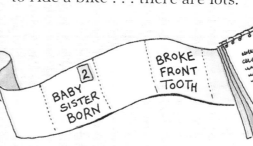

6. Mark your list on your time chart, then create names to describe those periods. What is the age before your first teeth — Pre-Toothian? What might the Gerbillian Age be?

Jurassic

Cretaceous

Diplodocus

Iguanodon

Triceratops

An interesting case of fossil detection

A few years ago, palaeontologists found some fossils of ammonites (squid-like animals that lived in the sea) with some unusual dents in their shells. Some of the dents actually went all the way through the shell. When they took a closer look, they found that the dents and holes were in a distinct pattern. What had caused the damage? The obvious solution to the mystery was that the ammonites had been bitten—but by whom? The damaged ammonites were late Cretaceous in age. Here was an important clue, because during that time there were some large swimming lizards in the sea called mosasaurs. A search was made for a likely culprit. Eventually a match was made between the tooth marks on the ammonites and the tooth pattern of a particular type of mosasaur. And so, by this careful piece of detective work, it was possible to name the type of reptile that had attacked these particular ammonites more than 65 million years ago. (For more about mosasaurs, see page 83.)

A helping hand from technology

Modern palaeontologists, like modern police detectives, use the latest technology to help them solve their cases. One useful piece of equipment is the CAT-scanner. This is a special X-ray machine used in hospitals to obtain pictures of imaginary slices cut through people. CAT-scans show much more detail than ordinary X-rays.

A CAT-scanner was recently used to find out whether an ichthyosaur called *Eurhinosaurus* had a tail. Ichthyosaurs were reptiles that lived in the sea. They looked very much like fish (for more about ichthyosaurs, see Chapter 7). Like fish, most ichthyosaurs had tails. But not all did. One palaeontologist suspected that *Eurhinosaurus* was one of the tailless sort, but how could this be confirmed when the fleshy part of the tail was not preserved?

Some detective work revealed that ichthyosaurs that have fish-like tails also have vertebrae (the bones of the vertebral column) of a particular shape (page 77). So if the shape of the vertebrae in the tail region could be discovered, the case could be closed.

The shape of the vertebrae could not be seen properly in any of the specimens of *Eurhinosaurus*. This is where the CAT-scanner came in. A specimen of *Eurhinosaurus* was taken to the local hospital and put inside a CAT-scan machine. The X-ray pictures showed the shape of vertebrae . . . *Eurhinosaurus* had a tail. The doctors at the hospital said that the 200-million-year-old fossil was their oldest patient!

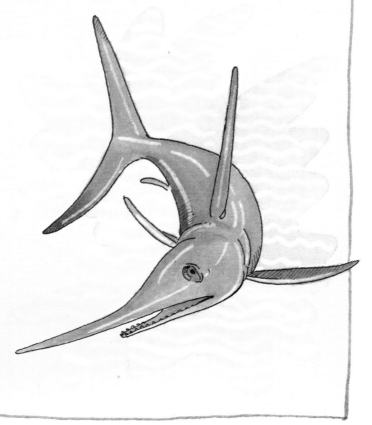

2. Clues in the ground: fossils

Fossils are the remains of old animals and plants, usually the hard parts, such as bones and shells and wood. The word "fossil" comes from a Latin word meaning "dug up," so if your dog digs up a nice juicy bone in the back yard, you could say that it has found a fossil. However, palaeontologists use the word fossil only for things that are thousands or millions of years old.

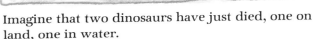

Imagine that two dinosaurs have just died, one on land, one in water.

Scavengers—animals that feed on dead bodies—set to work on the first dinosaur. These scavengers range from meat-eating dinosaurs to small insects.

The dinosaur that died in water begins to rot and sinks to the bottom of the river.

Months later. All that remains of the land dinosaur is a scattering of bones, most of them crunched and broken by scavengers. The bones crack and flake away under the heat of the sun.

The dinosaur that died in water has rotted away to a skeleton, which becomes covered by the sediments that settle on the river bottom as mud.

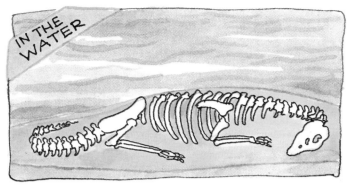

A few years later. Nothing is left of the first dinosaur but a few scraps of bone, some of which have been partly buried by soil.

Sediments continue to accumulate over the skeleton on the river bottom.

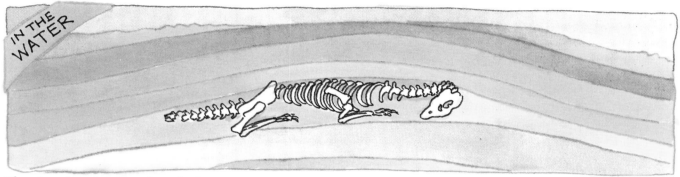

The river has dried up but the build-up of sediments carries on, though much more slowly. The increased pressure crushes the dinosaur skeleton and causes the sediments to turn to rock. Groundwater containing minerals seeps into the bones. Minerals from the water collect in the small spaces of the bone, making the bone much heavier and harder.

Quick burial is the key to becoming a fossil because it stops scavengers from doing their work. The chances of quick burial are much higher in water than on land. This explains why fossils of sea animals are much more common than those of land animals.

Tens of millions of years later. Erosion of the rocks and the movements of the Earth's crust cause the layer containing the dinosaur skeleton to become exposed. A palaeontologist just happens to be in the right place at the right time and sees some pieces of bone. If the skeleton is not collected, it will eventually be destroyed by erosion—the wearing away of the rocks and fossils by the weather.

When you think of fossils, you probably think of skeletons, especially the big dinosaur skeletons you see in museums. But bones are not the only kinds of fossils. Sometimes fossils of animal footprints are found imprinted in the rock. Try the activity "Faking a fossil footprint" on this page to see how they were made.

Occasionally the impressions of animal skin are found. How does skin become a fossil? Imagine an animal lying down on the soft ground. The weight of the animal, especially if it is big and heavy like a dinosaur, presses the skin into the ground, leaving an impression. Later the impression gets filled with sand or soil, which hardens and becomes a natural copy, or cast, of the skin. Try making "dinosaur skin" by following the instructions on pages 24–25.

Sometimes dinosaur skin casts are found with skeletons, as in this hadrosaur specimen at the Royal Ontario Museum. This tells us that hadrosaurs had a pebbly skin, something like that of a modern elephant.

COURTESY OF THE ROYAL ONTARIO MUSEUM, TORONTO, CANADA.

ACTIVITY

Faking a fossil footprint

Most fossil footprints are formed when the ground over which an animal has walked becomes hard. Over thousands of years, the ground slowly changes into rock so the footprint becomes permanent. You can speed up the fossilization process and fake a footprint.

You'll need:
- *a cup-sized container filled with damp sand*
- *a co-operative cat or dog (if you can't get one, don't worry)*
- *nail polish (clear is best)*
  Warning: Nail polish must be used in a well-ventilated room.
- *an old toothbrush or paintbrush*

1. Press down the sand with your fingers until it's level.

2. Gently press one of your pet's feet into the sand, just hard enough to make an impression. If you don't have a pet, use your thumb instead.

The impressions of delicate objects, such as leaves, and the bodies of soft animals, such as worms, shrimps, and even jellyfish, are sometimes preserved. But the most likely things to be preserved are the hard parts of animals—the bones and shells —and the wood of plants.

COURTESY OF THE ROYAL ONTARIO MUSEUM, TORONTO, CANADA.

3. Drip the nail polish in and around the imprint. You'll probably need less than a teaspoon of polish and be sure to use it in a well-ventilated room. The polish will soak into the sand, sticking it together. This is a sped-up version of the natural process of sand becoming sandstone.

4. Leave your print overnight for the nail polish to harden.

5. Remove your "sandstone" print by loosening the sand all around it.

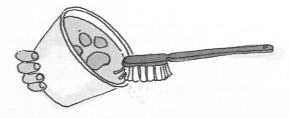

6. Gently remove the loose sand from the back of the impression using the toothbrush.

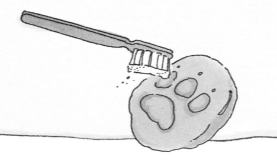

ACTIVITY

Faking dinosaur skin

You'll need:

- an old newspaper
- dry sand—about 10 mL (2 teaspoons)
- an old pair of pantyhose
- a cup
- a spoon
- the lid of a shoe box or an old dinner plate
- damp soil (enough to fill the lid or plate)
- an empty bottle (choose one with no curves in the middle)
- a corn cob
- nail polish (clear is best)
  Warning: Nail polish must be used in a well-ventilated room.
- an old table knife (a plastic one will do)
- an old toothbrush or a paintbrush

1. Spread the newspaper out over your work area to keep things clean.

2. Remove the lumps in the dry sand. To do this, stretch a piece of old pantyhose over an old cup and use this as a sieve. Rub the sand through the mesh with the back of a spoon. Set the lump-free sand aside.

3. Fill the lid or plate with the damp soil, then roll the soil flat with the bottle.

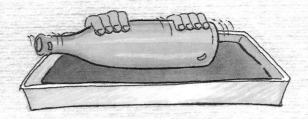

4. Remove the husk from the corn as if you were going to cook the ear.

5. Firmly press the corn cob into the soil, rocking it slightly from side to side to get a good impression. When you remove the cob, you should be able to see a clear imprint showing several rows of kernels. A corn cob has a pebbled surface, something like that of dinosaur skin.

6. Carefully sprinkle the lump-free sand into the impression so it forms a thin layer over all the pits and ridges. The finer the sand and the more carefully you do this, the better the result will be.

7. Once you have sprinkled enough sand into the impression to cover the soil, the rest of the sand can be added quickly. Stop adding sand when it has reached the level of the soil.

8. Drip nail polish onto the sand so that it soaks in and glues all the particles together. Leave to dry and harden for one or two days.

9. When your artificial sandstone feels hard, loosen the soil all around it with the knife and lift it free. Carefully scrape away the soil with the knife. Stop scraping as soon as you reach the sand. (If your "sandstone" feels soft, let it harden for another day.) Remove the last of the soil with the brush. If this doesn't work, hold it under a tap and let cold water trickle on the soil while you gently rub it away with your fingers. Palaeontologists do the same sort of thing when they remove the sediments from a real fossil.

FOSSIL HUNTING

How would you like to go out hunting for dinosaurs? Finding even a part of a dinosaur skeleton is a bit like finding a needle in a haystack. For starters, you have to know where to look. Fossils are usually found in rocks, but not just any old rocks. They're found in layered, or "sedimentary," rocks. These rocks were formed when small particles, such as sand and soil, settled in seas, lakes, rivers and on land. The layers of particles gradually became pressed together, eventually hardening into rocks.

There are lots of sedimentary rocks around the world, but they're often covered over by soil and plants. So palaeontologists have to go where the rocks are exposed, places such as cliffs, deserts, mountains and along canyons cut by rivers. These locations are often in remote areas that are difficult to reach.

It's very unlikely you'd find an uncovered skeleton, and if you did, it would be so badly broken up by weathering that it probably wouldn't be worth collecting. What palaeontologists look for are pieces of bone peeping through the rock. Sometimes they spend days at a time tramping over rocks without finding anything. And when bone is sighted, it's more likely to be a single bone, or just a few bones, than a whole skeleton.

Suppose you've been lucky enough to find a piece of dinosaur bone sticking out of the rock. What happens next? The hard work begins—you and your helpers have to dig and chop away at the rock to find out what's there. If the rock is fairly soft, you can use picks and shovels. But it may be as hard as concrete, so you have to use jackhammers.

Once all the specimen has been cleared of rock—and it can take a team of six people from a few days to a few weeks to do this—the skeleton has to be collected. Instead of freeing the individual bones from the rock, which would take far too long, the bones are collected in blocks that are cut out from the rest of the rock. The blocks are then specially wrapped to protect the bones from being damaged during transportation back to the museum. The wrapping method used today is the same as was used by the pioneer dinosaur hunters of the 1800s. The exposed bones are first covered with tissue paper. Then strips of burlap (sacking cloth) are dipped in wet plaster and used to bandage up the block. When the plaster has set, the field jackets, as they are called, are labelled with a marker and put into crates.

Once the field jackets are back at the museum, they are cut open to reveal the bones. Technicians then set to work with various tools to clear the rock from the bones. This process is called "preparation." It may take one technician a year or more to prepare a single dinosaur skeleton.

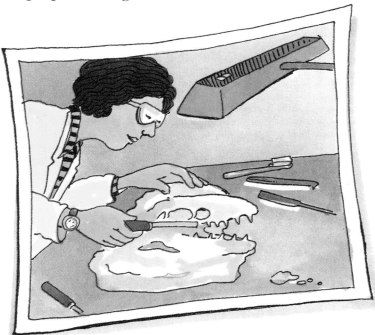

EXPERIMENT
Buried bones

Millions of dinosaurs once roamed the Earth. They must have left behind billions of bones when they died, yet finding dinosaur bones is very rare. Why? Find out one reason why with this experiment. This is a long-term experiment that should be started during the spring, as soon as the ground is frost free. The experiment will run until late fall.

You'll need:
- *clean chicken bones (see page 91, steps 2 and 3)*
- *a garden trowel*
- *a stick, plastic knitting needle or a long nail*
- *a metre (yard) of strong sewing thread*
- *a magnifying glass or binoculars (to use binoculars as a microscope, simply use them in reverse, hold an eyepiece close to the object and look through the other end)*

1. Check over your bones and make up pairs. For example, a pair of thigh bones (femora), a pair of shin bones (tibiae) and a pair of ribs. (Use long bones, not vertebrae.) Use only bones that are undamaged.

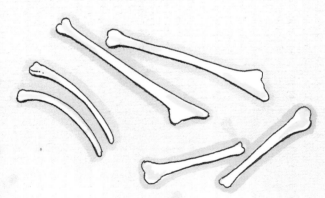

2. Make up two sets of bones, choosing one from each pair for each set. Make a list of the bones that are in each set so that you can see whether any are missing at the end of the experiment.

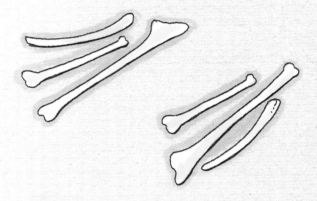

3. Choose a sunny spot in your yard or a vacant lot. Dig a hole about 12 cm (5 inches) deep and put one set of bones into the hole. Cover with soil and press the soil down firmly. Mark the spot with the stick.

4. Take one of the bones from the other set and tie it to one end of the thread. Tie the other end to a nearby bush or tree— as if it were a dog on a leash. Place the tied-up bone on top of the buried bones. Put the rest of the bones beside the tied-up bone.

5. Inspect the uncovered bones every week. Make notes of any changes or disappearances.

6. Before the ground freezes at the start of winter, dig up the buried bones. Wash off both sets of bones with cold water. Dab them dry with tissues. Compare the buried bones with the surface bones for cracks and breaks. Check their surfaces using the magnifier.

Did all the surface bones, except the tethered one, disappear? What do you think happened to them?

The buried bones are probably darker in colour than the surface ones and probably feel much smoother. Look closely with a magnifier and you'll probably notice that the unburied bone is rougher than its buried partner. Surface bones soon crack and flake when exposed to the sun. This is why they eventually break up and disappear even without the help of scavengers.

3. What did dinosaurs eat?

Suppose you are a palaeontologist who has found this complete dinosaur skeleton. Palaeontologists usually find only bits of a skeleton, but you've been incredibly lucky: you've found the whole thing. And suppose the dinosaur you've just unearthed is something new—a type that nobody had ever seen before.

Take a good look at your new discovery. Can you read the bony clues and tell what this dinosaur ate? You can, with a bit of detective work.

Let's start with the mouth. What can you tell about this dinosaur by looking at its teeth and jaws? Can you guess what kinds of food it ate? Knowing what a dinosaur ate can tell you a lot about how it lived.

CLUES IN THE MOUTH

The most important clues to an animal's diet are its teeth. What sort of teeth does your new dinosaur have? They are sharply pointed, like daggers, and if you look very closely, you'll see they have cutting edges, like steak knives.

You don't have to be a Sherlock Holmes to deduce that those teeth were probably used for slicing through meat. You can also deduce that your dinosaur had a powerful bite because the lower jaw and the skull are both deep (that is, it's wide, from top to bottom), as in modern-day meat eaters such as lions, dogs and cats. Deep jaws not only give lots of room for the attachment of large jaw muscles, but they also provide deep sockets for the long roots of the teeth. The teeth have to be firmly rooted to prevent them from being pulled out during struggles with their prey. Your dinosaur was obviously a meat eater, or "carnivore." For more bony clues to dinosaurs' meat-eating ways, see pages 36 and 38.

EXPERIMENT
Are you a carnivore?

You may prefer meat to vegetables but that does not make you a carnivore. If you tried sinking your teeth into a wild buffalo, you'd soon discover your teeth aren't sharp enough for the job.

1. Run the tip of your tongue over your teeth. Notice that they are all about the same length and none sticks out much farther than any of the others. If you have a mirror, you can see this for yourself.
2. Open wide and gently close your teeth on your forearm, as shown. Bite down (very gently) on the meaty part of your arm, not a bony part.
3. Slowly increase the force of your bite. Does it hurt? Not all that much because your teeth are all at about the same level so the pressure is applied evenly.

4. Look at the marks left on your arm by your teeth. The marks are all about the same depth — more evidence that your teeth are all about the same length.

If you had been a carnivorous mammal, this would have been a painful experiment. This is because carnivores have some extra-long teeth, called canine teeth, that extend well beyond the level of the others. Canine teeth are sharply pointed and are mainly used for killing prey. You have canine teeth too, but they are quite blunt. Do you know which ones they are? Put your finger on the gap between your two front teeth — either the upper ones or the lower ones. Now move your finger along to the left or to the right, counting off the teeth as you go. The third tooth along is your canine tooth.

To see how carnivores use their teeth, watch a dog with a meaty bone. Dogs use their front teeth (incisors) to tear off bits of sinew and meat from the bone, and their cheek teeth for slicing and gnawing. They often hold their head on one side while chewing, to position the meat between their cheek teeth. The slicing action of the teeth works well because there is no side-to-side movement of the jaws. If there were any sideways movement, chewing would be like trying to cut cardboard with a pair of

scissors that had a loose joint. Instead of the blades of the scissors sliding past each other and cutting cleanly, they would wobble from side to side, jamming the cardboard between the blades. We can waggle our lower jaw from side to side but carnivores can't.

33

STAB, SLICE AND GRIND

Plant eaters, or "herbivores," do not need the stabbing and slicing teeth of carnivores. Instead, they need teeth that are good for grinding. Why? Plants are very tough and have to be ground up thoroughly before being swallowed. Herbivores' teeth grind in two ways: side to side and up and down. Your teeth can also grind in two ways but you're not as good at grinding up plants as herbivores are. One reason is that the grinding surfaces of your teeth are fairly flat, while those of herbivores have sharp ridges that act like files. These ridges are formed because the white outer layer of the tooth—the enamel—is much harder than the bony dentine below. As the dentine is worn down, sharp ridges of enamel remain. These ridges are great for grinding.

The tooth at the right belongs to a rabbit, a herbivore. The tooth below is a human tooth.

ACTIVITY
Scientific ice cream

You can see how herbivores' teeth wear down next time you eat an ice-cream cone.

You'll need:
○ *an ice-cream cone (choose smooth ice cream—no nuts or raisins)*

1. Lick away at the ice cream until it is level with the edge of the cone.

2. Take several more licks, then examine your ice cream. Because the ice cream is much softer than the cone, it wears down faster. The ice cream becomes hollowed out, surrounded by a ridge of cone. In much the same way, the dentine of a herbivore's tooth becomes hollowed out, surrounded by a ridge of enamel.

Meat or veggies?

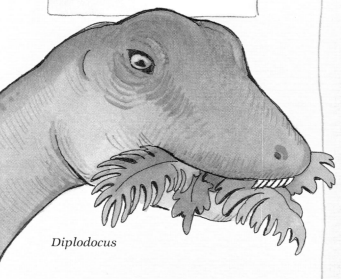

Diplodocus

Although you see a lot of pictures of dinosaurs attacking other dinosaurs, the truth is that most were herbivores. *Diplodocus* and all its long-necked relatives were herbivores; so too were the horned dinosaurs such as *Triceratops*; the armoured dinosaurs; the plated dinosaurs; and all the duck-bill dinosaurs and iguanodons. These herbivores provided food for the carnivores (meat eaters).

If you went on safari to Africa, you'd see lots of different herbivore species— zebras, antelopes, wildebeests, gazelles —but relatively few species of carnivores, such as lions. The numbers of lions would also be smaller than the number of individuals in any of the herbivore species. Why? There are lots of plant eaters because there are lots of plants for them to eat. However, if there were lots of carnivores, too, they would soon eat up all the herbivores and run out of food.

Hunter or scavenger?

Just because an animal is a carnivore doesn't mean that it hunts and kills for food. The present-day lion is a carnivore that hunts and kills, but the hyena, which also eats meat, gets most of its food by eating animals that are already dead. This is called being a scavenger. When lions have made a kill, hyenas are often seen lurking around in small packs, hoping for a chance to get at the lions' meal. Although hyenas spend much of their time scavenging, they also do some hunting of their own.

Some palaeontologists think that *Tyrannosaurus* and its relatives were scavengers that never hunted. Other palaeontologists think they scavenged and hunted. Animals that hunt other animals are called predators. Although we can never be completely sure, there are clues in the skeleton to show whether an animal was likely a predator. Let's take another look at the dinosaur bones you discovered for some clues.

Tyrannosaurus

35

EYE CLUES

The position of the eyes is a clue to whether a dinosaur was a predator.

Eyes that face forward—like cats' and dogs' and ours—are good for judging distances. This is very important for helping a hunter capture its prey. Having eyes that face forward means that the animal probably has binocular vision (binocular means "two-at-a-time eyes"). Can you think of any other animals that have binocular vision? Lions and wolves do, and so do other predators such as birds of prey (owls, hawks, eagles). Having binocular vision helps these animals catch their prey.

Eyes that face sideways, like a rabbit's, aren't good for hunting. But sideways-looking eyes are good for all-around vision. This is useful for animals that are hunted—it enables them to watch for predators sneaking up on them.

What sort of eyes do you think your dinosaur had? You can get some idea of whether they faced forward or sideways by looking at the illustration on the left and checking the placement of the eye sockets, or orbits. Was your dinosaur a hunter or the hunted? What about these dinosaurs? Based on the placement of the orbits, which do you think were predators and which were prey? (Answers page 96.)

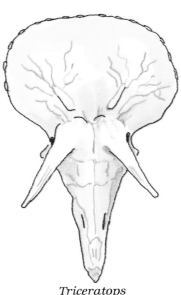

Triceratops

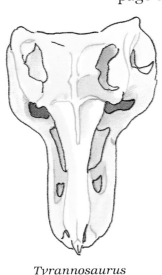

Tyrannosaurus

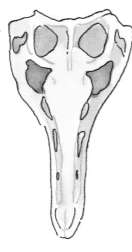

Nanotyrannus

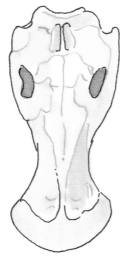

Edmontosaurus

36

EXPERIMENT
How much can you see?

Animals that hunt have eyes that face forward. Animals that are hunted have their eyes at the sides of their heads. This gives them the best possible all-around vision. Why? The answer has to do with the visual angle of the eye. The visual angle is how much an eye can see on either side of it. How big is the visual angle of each of your eyes? Try this and see. All you need is a small piece of tissue.

1. Put a postage-stamp-sized piece of wet tissue on a wall at eye level. Take a giant step away from the wall and face the tissue.

2. Close your left eye and stare hard at the tissue. Stretch your right arm out to the side so you can't see it when you're staring at the tissue.

3. Wiggle the fingers of your right hand and slowly move your arm forward. Keep staring at the tissue with your right eye. As soon as you see your fingers out of the corner of your eye, stop moving your arm.

4. Stretch out your left arm and point at the tissue. What is the approximate angle between your two arms? You have measured half the visual angle of just your right eye. To measure the other half, you would need to repeat the experiment with your left arm stretched out at the side. However, this doesn't work because your nose gets in the way. (Try it and see!) So to get your whole visual angle, simply double the angle you already found.

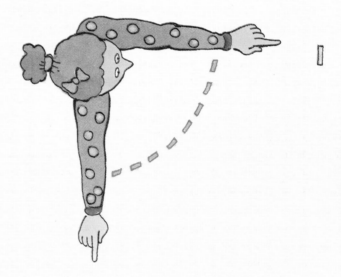

Your visual angle is almost a half-circle (180°). Most other animals have similar visual angles. A horse, with eyes on the sides of its head, could see almost a full circle without moving its head. Predators (hunters) are different. Because their eyes face forward, the visual angles of their two eyes overlap. This overlap gives them the binocular vision so useful in hunting.

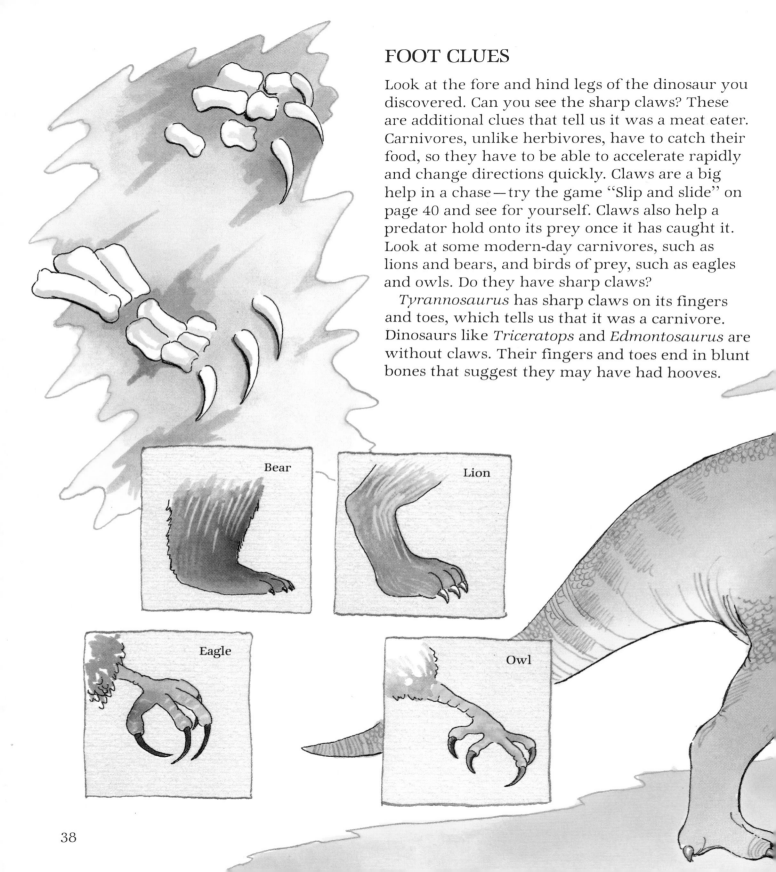

FOOT CLUES

Look at the fore and hind legs of the dinosaur you discovered. Can you see the sharp claws? These are additional clues that tell us it was a meat eater. Carnivores, unlike herbivores, have to catch their food, so they have to be able to accelerate rapidly and change directions quickly. Claws are a big help in a chase—try the game "Slip and slide" on page 40 and see for yourself. Claws also help a predator hold onto its prey once it has caught it. Look at some modern-day carnivores, such as lions and bears, and birds of prey, such as eagles and owls. Do they have sharp claws?

Tyrannosaurus has sharp claws on its fingers and toes, which tells us that it was a carnivore. Dinosaurs like *Triceratops* and *Edmontosaurus* are without claws. Their fingers and toes end in blunt bones that suggest they may have had hooves.

Bear

Lion

Eagle

Owl

Triceratops

Tyrannosaurus

Terrible claw

In the mid-1960s a new dinosaur was discovered in Montana that caused a lot of excitement. Its sharp teeth and sharp claws showed it was a carnivore, but when its feet were examined a remarkable discovery was made. Not only was the claw of the inside toe (the equivalent of the toe next to our big toe) twice as large as the others, but one of the toe joints was a special joint, like a cat's, that allowed the dinosaur to draw in its claws when not in use. Withdrawing the claws helped to keep them sharp. The Montana dinosaur also had a stiff straight tail and an unusual pelvis. Palaeontologists think these features helped it to balance on one foot while slashing at its unfortunate victims with the big claw of the other foot. This remarkable dinosaur, only about 3.4 m (11 feet) long, was named *Deinonychus*, which means "terrible claw."

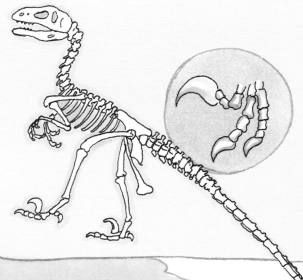

ACTIVITY
Slip and slide

You'll need:
- *friends with "clawed feet" (running shoes)*
- *a large room with a polished floor —a school gym is ideal*

1. Choose somebody to be "It." This player takes off his or her running shoes and plays in sock feet.

2. The sock-footed player tries to tag the others. Your sock-footed friend will probably find it impossible to tag anyone wearing running shoes. She'll slip and slide all over the place. Try changing players and see if anyone else can do any better in just socks. Running shoes improve a person's grip on the ground and allow fast direction changes.

Claws do the same thing for some animals. When predators are hunting, they need claws to help them make quick changes in direction and keep up with their prey.

EXPERIMENT
Arms and armour

Triceratops

Horns, plates and tail-clubs allowed some dinosaurs to defend themselves against predators. Some, like *Triceratops*, had large horns on their heads that were probably used to defend themselves. Ankylosaurs, such as *Euoplocephalus*, were heavily built with thick bony plates embedded in their skin. These plates would have been difficult even for a tyrannosaur to bite through. They also had a surprise for attackers—a heavy, bony club at the end of their tail. A blow from the club might even have broken bones. It would certainly have hurt!

How effective were the bony plates of ankylosaurs in defending them against attack? Turn a potato into an ankylosaur and find out.

2. Carefully chop at the unprotected surface of the potato. Use just enough force to cut through the skin. Make two or three cuts.

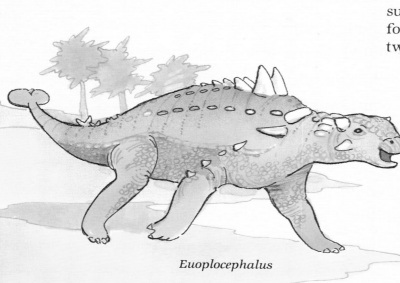

Euoplocephalus

3. Using the same amount of force, chop at the cardboard plates.

You'll need:
- 2 straight pins
- 2 squares of cardboard (about 2.5 cm or 1 inch square)
- a large potato
- a blunt table knife

1. Using the pins, attach the squares (or "plates") to the potato.

4. Increase the force of your chops to the plates until you mark the skin below. Did you have to use a lot more force? (Save your potato and re-use it in the experiment on page 59.)

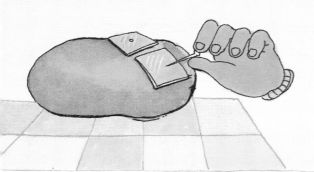

41

4. How did dinosaurs move?

Tyrannosaurus

Ornithomimus

Triceratops

Stegosaurus

What do you notice about the way these dinosaurs walk? They've all got four legs, but two of them walk on two legs, like you do, while the other three walk on all four, like cats and dogs. Walking on two legs is called being bipedal, which means "two feet." *Ornithomimus* and *Tyrannosaurus* were bipedal. Walking on all fours is called being quadrupedal, which means "four feet." *Diplodocus*, *Triceratops* and *Stegosaurus* were quadrupedal.

No one has ever seen a dinosaur walk, so how do palaeontologists know whether a dinosaur was bipedal or quadrupedal? They look at the bones. The first clue is leg size. Bipedal dinosaurs usually have back legs that are much longer than their front legs. But in most quadrupedal dinosaurs, the difference in lengths is much less.

The second clue is in the tail. Bipedal dinosaurs usually have tails that are longer than the rest of their body. They need the tail for balance. Most quadrupedal dinosaurs have tails that are shorter than the rest of their body. (There are

exceptions, however: some quadrupedal dinosaurs, such as *Diplodocus*, have very long tails.)

How did bipedal dinosaurs balance themselves on their back legs alone? It all has to do with the centre of mass. The centre of mass (some-

times called the centre of gravity) is the balance point of a body. If you laid a ruler across your finger so that it balanced, your finger would be right under the centre of mass of the ruler.

As long as a dinosaur (or any other animal) keeps its

Diplodocus

centre of mass between the feet that are on the ground, it won't fall over. You can pretend you're a dinosaur and try it for yourself. Before you do, you've got to find out where your centre of mass is. See the box on the right for how to do this.

EXPERIMENT
Finding your centre of mass

Here's an easy way of finding your centre of mass: with your hand flat and thumb and fingers together, place your hand on your stomach so that your thumb touches your navel. Your centre of mass is about at the level of your little finger. Mark the spot on your body with a piece of masking tape.

Here's another way to find your centre of mass —it's a bit more complicated but a lot more fun.

You'll need:
○ *a smooth floor*
○ *a plank of wood that is about as long as you are tall (a piece of two-by-four works well)*
○ *a round piece of wood, about 2 cm ($\frac{3}{4}$ inch) in diameter (a broom handle or a piece of dowel works well)*
○ *an assistant*
○ *masking tape*

1. Balance the plank on the piece of wood, like a teeter-totter.
2. Lie down on the plank so that the top of your head and your heels are about the same distance from either end. Press your arms against your sides. You'll probably find that the head end of the plank touches the floor.
3. Ask your assistant to roll the round piece of wood towards the head end of the plank as you continue to lie on it. When your body balances, the round piece of wood will be right under your centre of mass. Get your assistant to mark your centre of mass by sticking a piece of tape on your body.

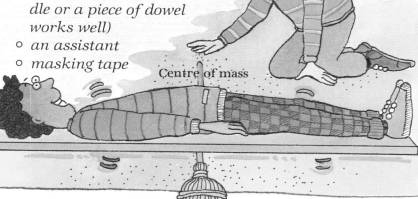

Centre of mass

EXPERIMENT

Be a quadrupedal (four-legged) dinosaur

You'll need:

- *a piece of elastic at least as long as you are*
- *a paper clip*
- *a piece of thread*
- *masking tape*

1. Tie the paper clip to the end of the thread. Use masking tape to attach the other end of the thread to your stomach, at the level of your centre of mass (see "Finding your centre of mass" on page 43). Adjust the length of the thread so that the paper clip hangs just below your knees.

2. Tie the ends of the elastic together.

3. Take off your shoes and socks and position yourself as shown. The elastic should form a rectangle and the paper clip should dangle in the middle of the rectangle, almost touching the floor.

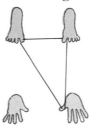

4. Leave your right hand where it is, but release the elastic from your right thumb. The elastic now forms a triangle between your left hand and your two feet. The paper clip falls just outside the triangle. This means that your centre of mass lies outside the triangle, too. That's okay as long as all four of your "feet" are on the ground. But what happens if you take your right hand off the floor?

Remember—as long as an animal keeps its centre of mass between the feet that are on the ground, it will not fall over. Try it and see.

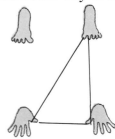

5. Get back onto all fours again, with the elastic forming a rectangle, as before. Taking care not to move your right foot, let go of the elastic with your right big toe. The paper clip falls inside the triangle this time. If you took your right foot off the ground, would you expect to topple? Check it out.

EXPERIMENT

Be a bipedal (two-legged) dinosaur

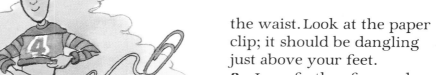

You'll need:

○ *a piece of thread long enough to reach from your waist to the floor*
○ *a paper clip*
○ *masking tape*
○ *a broom or a mop*

1. Tie one end of the thread to the paper clip. Use the masking tape to attach the other end to your body, at the level of your centre of mass. Adjust the length of the thread so that the paper clip reaches your toes.

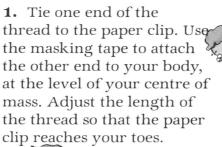

2. With your hands held behind your back, lean forward, bending slightly at the waist. Look at the paper clip; it should be dangling just above your feet.

3. Lean farther forward. What happens?

4. Repeat Step 3, but this time hold the broom out behind you as if it were a tail. Can you lean a little farther forward this time before you start toppling? Your "tail" is helping you to balance.

5. Let go of the broom. What happens?

Bipedal dinosaurs had long tails to balance the weight of the front part of their bodies. Can you think of a modern animal that uses its tail to help it walk (or, in this case, hop) on two legs?

HOW FAST COULD DINOSAURS RUN?

Some dinosaurs could run faster than others. *Stegosaurus*, for example, was probably slow and lumbering, while hadrosaurs, such as *Lambeosaurus*, could probably run quite quickly. How can palaeontologists tell whether dinosaurs ran quickly or slowly? After all, they've been extinct for more than 65 million years! The clues are in the legs.

Which of the two legs below do you think could run faster? If you said the one on the right, congratulations. It belongs to a horse and horses are speedy. The other leg belongs to an elephant, which is a much slower runner.

Look where the knees are. The elephant's knee is in about the middle of its leg. The horse's knee is higher up; there's more leg below the knee than above it. There's an important clue here. Animals whose lower legs are longer than their thighs (upper legs) are the faster runners. The same is true for dinosaurs. If you compare the positions of the knees in the illustrations on the right, you'll see why *Lambeosaurus* was probably a faster runner than *Stegosaurus*.

Another thing that affects how quickly or slowly an animal moves is inertia. What's inertia? Inertia is the tendency for things to stay where they are. Ask a friend to sit in a chair, then try pushing it across the floor—whew! If your friend gets out of the chair, it's much easier to push. By reducing the weight, you've reduced the inertia.

When animals move, they have to overcome the inertia of their limbs. The greater the inertia, the harder their muscles have to work, just as you had to work harder to push a chair with someone sitting in it. Anything that reduces the inertia not only cuts down on the amount of work that the muscles have to do, it also increases the speed of the limbs. Reduce inertia, increase speed. Imagine trying to run with rocks in your socks. Remove the rocks and you'd speed up.

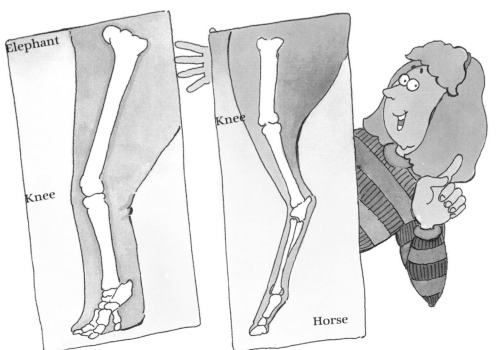

Stegosaurus

Elephant

Knee

Knee

Horse

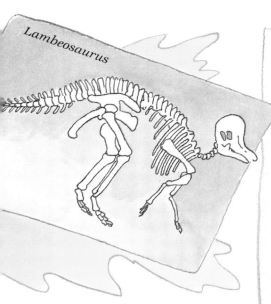

Lambeosaurus

Fast runners often have more lightly built legs than slower runners. Compare the thick, heavy-looking limbs of *Stegosaurus* on page 42 with the thin, lightly built limbs of *Ornithomimus* on page 42. The inertia of the legs of *Stegosaurus* would have been huge compared with *Ornithomimus*, so it would have been much slower moving.

Another way of reducing the inertia of a leg is to have most of the weight of the leg positioned as close to the hip joint as possible. Trained athletes, when they are running, do this by lifting their feet up high when they take them off the ground. Animals that run fast do the same thing. Take a close look next time you see runners on TV or at a sporting event.

EXPERIMENT
Inertia race

You'll need:
- kitchen scales
- a pair of heavy winter boots
- a pair of sneakers
- some large stones
- a watch
- a helper

1. Weigh the boots and the sneakers separately. Calculate the difference in weight between them. If the boots weigh .5 kg (1 pound) and the shoes weigh .25 kg ($\frac{1}{2}$ pound) the difference is
$5 - .25 = .25$ kg
$(1 - \frac{1}{2} = \frac{1}{2}$ pound).
Weigh out enough stones to equal the difference in weight between the boots and the sneakers.

2. Put on the boots and run 50 m (55 yards) while your helper times you.

3. Swap the boots for the sneakers and fill your pockets with the weighed stones. Repeat your run.

You'll find that you can run much faster in sneakers than in boots, even though the amount of extra weight you have to carry is the same. This is because adding weight to your feet increases the inertia of your legs far more than adding weight to your thighs (in your pocket).

CLUES FROM FOOTPRINTS

Footprints can give us some valuable clues as to how dinosaurs moved. Although we can't tell which dinosaur made a particular print, we can usually tell what sort of dinosaur it was. The meat-eating theropods, for example, left behind distinctive prints with three well-separated toe impressions. Each of their toes ended in a sharp claw, and impressions of these claws are often found just in front of the toe print. Theropod footprints are so similar to those of birds that it is sometimes difficult to tell them apart. Hadrosaurs also made three-toed prints with their hind feet, but the toe impressions are much broader and the footprints look more leaf-shaped than arrow-shaped.

Hunting for dinosaur tracks can be exciting and full of surprises. Let's go back to November 1938. Roland Bird, a palaeontologist with the American Museum of Natural History, heard about some unusual dinosaur footprints found along the Paluxy River in Texas. These trackways were imprinted in rock buried beneath the mud from the river. Bird was especially interested in track-ways, so he decided to take a look.

He didn't find anything unusual at first. There were two sets of tracks, probably made by a pair of large carnivorous dinosaurs walking close together. Bird collected these footprints by cutting out the slabs of stone that contained them. Then he began clearing away the mud from an area about a metre (yard) wide all around where he had been digging to make sure he hadn't missed any other footprints. As he shovelled, he discovered a round pot-hole about a metre (yard) across, filled with mud.

"When I dug into it and threw back a few shovelfuls for a look-see, my heart nearly jumped out of my mouth. There, right at my very feet, was a depression totally unlike any I had ever seen before, but one I instantly surmised must be a sauropod footprint."

Bird had indeed found a sauropod footprint—the

ACTIVITY
Sherlock Holmes in the snow

This detective game is played in snow with three friends. One stays inside while the other two set off in the snow, one walking, one jogging. They should cross paths at least once. Afterwards, the person indoors examines the tracks and deduces who went first and who moved faster.

No snow where you are? Try deducing what went on here. The solution is on page 96.

first to be discovered—and he correctly identified it as having been made by a right hind foot. By heading in the direction in which the toes pointed, he tried to find the next print by the same foot. With mounting excitement, he shovelled at the mud, hoping to uncover that next print. And what did he find? Nothing!

He cleared more and more mud away and eventually hit the rim of the next depression. He was amazed to find that it was 4 m (13 feet) in front of the first one. Now that's a stride!

He returned the following year with a field crew and began digging up the trackways. At that time most palaeontologists believed that sauropods lived in water because they were too heavy to walk on land. But Bird found clues that they *did* walk on land. What were these clues?

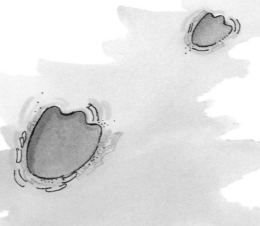

The first clue was that the prints were deep. If the sauropods had been walking in deep water, they would have been buoyed up and would not have made such deep footprints. The second clue is that scrolls of mud had been squeezed out at the sides of the feet as the weight of the animal pressed down on the ground. If the dinosaurs had been wading in water, these scrolls would have been washed away. So they must have been walking on land, probably on soft ground.

The prints made by the front feet were smaller and shallower than those made by the back feet, showing that most of the sauropod's weight was carried by the back legs. This means that a sauropod's centre of mass was towards its back end rather than its front. In the modern elephant, it's the other way around; their front feet are larger than the hind ones and most of the weight is carried by the front legs. Can you figure out why? If you said it's because of the large size of the elephant's head, you would be absolutely right. Would you believe that the head of an African elephant weighs three-quarters of a tonne (ton)?

The footprints Roland Bird discovered were so numerous in one area that they overlapped. Twenty-three separate sets were identified. Since they all pointed in the same direction and appear to have been made at the same time, it seems likely that the sauropods were travelling together as a group. And mixed in with the sauropod tracks were the unmistakable tracks of some large carnivores (meat eaters). Some of these lay beneath the sauropod tracks, showing that the carnivores had travelled along the route *before* the herd of sauropods. Were the carnivores waiting in ambush for the sauropods farther along the way? Other carnivore tracks crossed over the sauropod prints. These predators had travelled the route *after* the sauropods. In one case, the track of a carnivore was imprinted alongside that of a sauropod. When the sauropod trackway swung to the left, the carnivore followed. Was the predator following the sauropod? Perhaps the herd was being stalked. Other predators may have been lying in ambush for them farther along the way. No one will ever know for certain, but it's fun playing detective with an event that occurred more than 100 million years ago.

EXPERIMENT
Measure your stride

The distance between one footprint and the next print by the same foot is the stride length. The bigger the stride length, the bigger the dinosaur. Stride length increases with speed, so some experts have tried to deduce dinosaurs' speeds from trackways. Measure your stride and see how speed changes it. Compare your stride length to that of someone bigger. Here's how to measure:

○ Winter: walk in fresh snow.
○ Summer: wet your feet and walk on dry sidewalk.
○ Anytime (indoors): wet your feet and walk on several metres (yards) of paper towels that you've rolled out and taped to the floor in several places.

You'll need:
○ *a tape measure*
○ *a pencil and paper*

1. Start walking—a few metres (yards) will do.
2. Now start running. Speed up quickly until you are running as fast as you can. When you're at top speed, slow down and stop. (If you're experimenting indoors, you may have to use two strips of paper towel, one for walking, the other for running.)
3. Measure your walking stride length by measuring from the heel of one left footprint to the heel of the next left footprint, both in the walking section. Record a few stride lengths in case they vary. Repeat for the running section.

Did speed change your stride length? If you compare your stride with that of someone larger or smaller, you'll find it also varies with size.

You may not be able to deduce a dinosaur's speed from stride lengths, but you can estimate how fast one dinosaur was moving compared with another. If there are two sections of trackway, both made by dinosaurs of similar size, the one with the longest stride length would have been travelling faster.

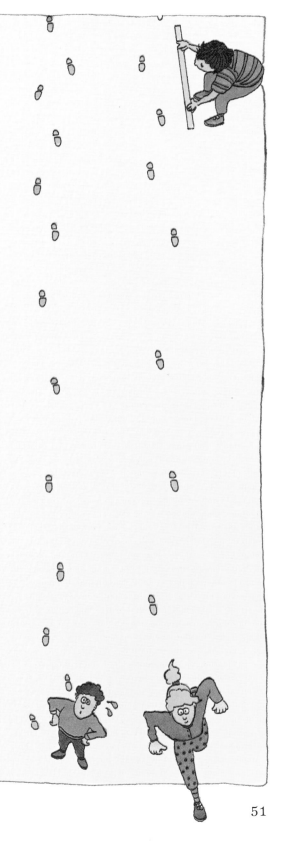

5. How big were dinosaurs?

Not all dinosaurs were big. Some dinosaurs, such as *Dromaeosaurus*, were the size of large dogs. *Compsognathus* was no bigger than a chicken. But most dinosaurs were B-I-G. The duck-bills (hadrosaurs), which were very common dinosaurs, weighed about 4 tonnes (tons). *Tyrannosaurus*, which probably preyed upon the hadrosaurs, weighed close to 8 tonnes (tons). (The largest land animal alive today, the African elephant, weighs only about 6 tonnes [tons].)

But *Tyrannosaurus* was a lightweight compared with the sauropods, which were all plant eaters. *Diplodocus*, one of the lighter sauropods, tipped the scales at 18 tonnes (tons), while *Apatosaurus* (which used to be called *Brontosaurus*) weighed 28 tonnes (tons) and *Brachiosaurus* weighed almost 80 tonnes (tons)—about the weight of a Boeing 727 airliner!

One day in 1907, a German geologist was prospecting for minerals in a remote part of

Dromaeosaurus

Compsognathus

Africa called Tendaguru. The area had not been explored before, and he collected all sorts of interesting rock samples. Then he discovered something amazing—some gigantic bones sticking out of the rocks. They were too big to collect, so he reported his discovery when he got back to base.

One of the people who heard about the bones was the famous German palaeontologist Professor Eberhard Fraas, who happened to be visiting the area at the time. He set off to investigate the new finds. It was a long, hot and tiring journey, but it was well worth it—Tendaguru was crammed full of dinosaur bones.

Professor Fraas collected some of the better specimens and returned to Germany with them. When other palaeontologists saw his finds, they organized a full-scale expedition to Tendaguru. There were no proper roads, so native porters had to carry everything to and from the site on foot. Over the next four years, more than 250 tonnes (tons) of dinosaur bones were collected and shipped back to Berlin. Several different sorts of dinosaurs were found, but the prize was an almost complete skeleton of *Brachiosaurus*, one of the biggest dinosaurs that ever roamed the earth. The skeleton was put together in the entrance hall of the Berlin museum and is still the largest mounted dinosaur skeleton in the world.

By studying the skeleton, it was possible to tell approximately how much *Brachiosaurus* weighed when it was alive. How do palaeontologists calculate a dinosaur's weight when all they have to work with are its bones?

Diplodocus

Apatosaurus

Tyrannosaurus

Lambeosaurus

The first step is to make a Plasticine model of the dinosaur in question, based on its skeleton. This involves making some educated guesses about how much muscle fleshed out the skeleton. The next step is to work out what the model would weigh if it were made of flesh and bone rather than of Plasticine. The last step is to work out how much bigger the real dinosaur was, and multiply the weight of the dinosaur model by this number. Let's say your model dinosaur weighed 2 kg ($4\frac{1}{2}$ pounds) and you figured out that the real dinosaur was 100 times bigger than the model. So your real dinosaur would weigh $2 \times 100 = 200$ kg (450 pounds), right? Wrong! It's not that simple because the weights of things, including dinosaurs, change much more quickly than their sizes. Suppose you had two objects of the same shape—say two apples—and one was twice as big as the other. How much heavier would the bigger one be? A lot more than twice as heavy. In fact, the bigger apple would weigh eight times more than the smaller one. Surprised? Try the experiment "Size and weight gains" and see for yourself why this is so.

EXPERIMENT
Size and weight gains

In this experiment, you're going to build some cubes out of sugar cubes. A cube is a box-shaped object whose six sides are all square and are all the same size. (The die that you roll when playing a board game is a cube.)

You'll need:
○ *a box of sugar cubes*

1. Place one cube on the table. What is its length and weight? You can measure it in sugar cubes. The cube is one sugar cube long and weighs one sugar cube.
2. Build a second cube, this one with a length of two. How many cubes did you need? Eight. Although this cube is two sugar cubes long, it weighs eight sugar cubes. This cube is only twice as big as the first cube but eight times as heavy.

3. Build a third cube, this one with a length of three. How many cubes did you need? Twenty-seven. This cube is three times bigger than the first one but it's 27 times heavier.

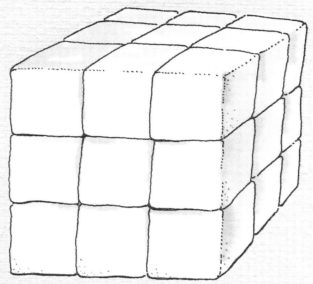

You can see that the weights of the cubes increase much faster than their lengths. But is there a pattern to the increase? The second cube was two times bigger than the first one, but its weight was two × two × two = eight times heavier. The third cube was three times bigger than the first one, but its weight was three × three × three = 27 times heavier. So, if you built a fourth cube that was four times bigger than the first one, it would weigh four × four × four = 64 times heavier. The pattern is: increase in weight = increase in size × increase in size × increase in size. Using this formula, try calculating the weight of your mom or dad. See "Weigh in" for how to do this.

ACTIVITY
Weigh in

Try calculating your parent's weight and see how close you come to the real weight.

You'll need:
- *a calculator*
- *height and weight information for one of your parents (preferably of the same sex as yourself)*
- *your own height and weight*

1. Find how much bigger your parent is than you. To do this, divide his or her height in centimetres or inches by your height. This gives you the increase in size.

2. Calculate his or her weight. To do this, multiply your weight by: increase in size × increase in size × increase in size.

How close were you? You probably found that your parent was a little heavier than you calculated. One of the reasons for this is that adults often have relatively more fat than children.

GIANT DINOSAURS

Next time you're at the zoo, take a look at the way elephants move. They don't do anything in a hurry. Notice how they keep their legs fairly straight when they walk. This reduces the stress on their leg bones. Watch an elephant's foot as it walks. The foot is large and flat and bulges out like a car tire when the elephant puts its weight on it. This is because of the thick spongy pad on the bottom of the foot, which acts as a cushion.

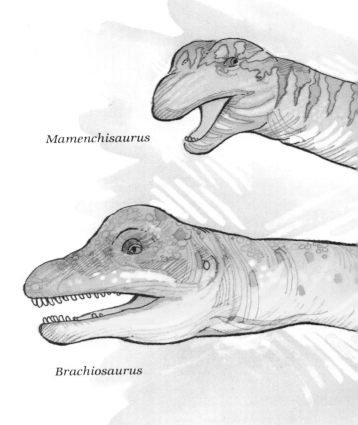

Mamenchisaurus

Brachiosaurus

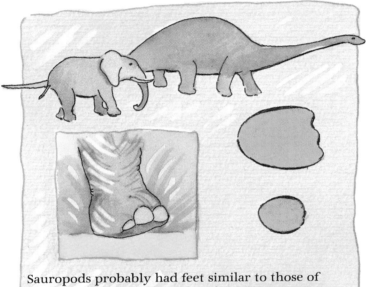

Sauropods probably had feet similar to those of elephants. How do we know? Look at the shape of their footprints.

Elephants may be big, but they are lightweights compared with some of the large sauropod dinosaurs. Imagine you were a *Brachiosaurus* weighing about 80 tonnes (tons). Think what an effort it would be just to move around. Each of your legs would weigh several tonnes (tons). You'd have to lift this huge weight and swing it forward every time you took a step. You wouldn't want to take up jogging! Being big could mean big trouble.

All sauropods had long necks. One sauropod, *Mamenchisaurus* from China, had a neck 10 m (33 feet) long—that's as long as a bus! A long neck could be very useful for reaching up into trees to nibble on leaves. But just think how hard the sauropod's heart had to work to pump blood all the way up that long neck to its head. A giraffe has the same problem. To overcome this, it has to pump blood out of its heart at very high pressure. A giraffe probably has the highest blood pressure of all living animals. The large sauropods had even longer necks, and it has been calculated that *Brachiosaurus* would have needed a blood pressure

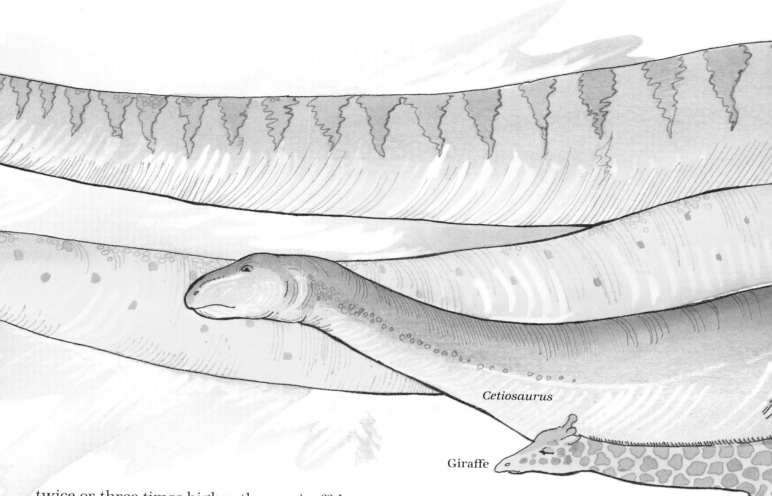

Cetiosaurus

Giraffe

twice or three times higher than a giraffe's. This seems an impossibly high blood pressure and would have required a heart weighing nearly two tonnes (tons), which seems unlikely. Palaeontologists have puzzled over this problem for some time. Then, in 1987, a possible solution was found in the skeleton of a sauropod called *Cetiosaurus*.

A palaeontologist in England was putting together a string of neck vertebrae (bones) of *Cetiosaurus* when he noticed something very interesting. When the neck vertebrae were assembled, they did not seem to have very much up-and-down movement. What if sauropods couldn't lift their necks high in the air as they are usually shown in

pictures? Then their hearts would not need to pump blood at such high pressures. This seems like a solution to the problem, but palaeontologists still have to check out the necks of other sauropods.

Being large wouldn't have been all bad news. For one thing, huge dinosaurs were probably left alone by meat-eating dinosaurs, just as elephants today are left alone by lions. Any lion crazy enough to tackle an elephant, which is about 30 times its own weight, is likely to be flattened! The larger dinosaurs, such as *Brachiosaurus*, probably would have been safe from predators for much the same reason. Their young, however, might not have been so lucky.

BODY SIZE AND BODY TEMPERATURES

One of the consequences of a dinosaur's large size was that its body would have stayed warm. This would have been true for all but the really small dinosaurs. Are you surprised to hear that dinosaurs had warm bodies? After all, dinosaurs were reptiles and reptiles are supposed to be cold-blooded, right? (See page 13 for more on this.)

Even though dinosaurs were reptiles, most of them had warm bodies because they were big. What has large size got to do with body temperature? Suppose a lizard and a squirrel were sitting in the noon-day sun. The lizard would have a similar body temperature to the squirrel because it has been warmed up by the sun. When night falls, the outside temperature drops. The squirrel maintains its body temperature during the night because of its higher metabolism, but the lizard cools down. How much it cools depends on its size. Large animals cool off more slowly than small ones, so dinosaurs would not have lost very much of their heat during the night. This is true today of the giant tortoises that live in the Galapagos Islands. They weigh about 200 kg (450 pounds)—small by dinosaur standards, but still big enough for them to keep much of their body heat during the night. As a result, they do not have to bask in the sun in the morning to raise their body temperatures. They stay fairly warm even though they have a low metabolism.

EXPERIMENT
Why big things stay warm

Why do big things cool off more slowly than small things? Heat is lost through surfaces—for example, you and other animals lose heat through your skin. Large things cool down much more slowly than small things simply because they've got relatively smaller surfaces through which to lose heat. Check this out for yourself.

You'll need:
- *an adult helper—do not do this experiment without adult supervision*
- *a saucepan*
- *2 potatoes, one large and one small (about 8 cm or 3 inches long and 4 cm or $1\frac{1}{2}$ inches long)*
- *a table knife*

1. Get your adult helper to boil some water in the saucepan and boil both of the potatoes for 25 minutes.

2. Get your adult helper to remove both potatoes from the saucepan and leave them to cool for 30 minutes.

3. Cut each potato in half and feel which one is coolest. Did the small potato cool off faster than the large one? The small potato has a much larger surface area (skin) for its size than the large one. Because of this, it cools faster. When you have a potato that's too hot to eat, you can cool it by cutting it into small pieces. Can you figure out why? Check your answer on page 96.

Metabolism—stoking up the fire

All animals produce heat inside their bodies. This heat comes from the chemical processes going on inside them and is called metabolism. Warm-blooded animals—birds and mammals—produce much more heat than cold-blooded ones; they have a higher metabolism. Having a high metabolism allows them to keep their bodies warm all the time. The cold-blooded animals—fish, amphibians, reptiles and most animals without backbones, such as ants and worms—have such a low metabolism they can't keep their bodies warm.

EXPERIMENT
Cool ants

Try cooling off some ants and see what happens to their activity levels.

You'll need:
- *10 ants*
- *2 small glass bottles with lids or stoppers*
- *permission to use a fridge in the cause of science*

1. Put five ants into each bottle and put the lid on.

2. Put one of the bottles in the fridge (not in the freezer!). This will be like sending the ants for a short winter holiday. Leave them there for two minutes.
3. At the end of the two minutes, remove the bottle from the fridge and look at the ants.

Which ants move more slowly? How soon are they all moving at the same speed? Why do you think they can change temperature so quickly? See page 96 for the answers.

What's so good about being warm-blooded?

The warmer an animal is, the more active it can be. Cold-blooded animals, such as lizards, are very sluggish at the start of the day and have to spend some time warming up in the sun before they can become active. Warm-blooded animals (mammals and birds) don't need to warm up in the sun; they make their own heat inside their bodies. This means they can be active whenever they want to be. If you had to run after your dinner—or run to avoid being someone else's dinner—you'd soon see why being active is so important!

Overheating

Elephants often get too hot, especially on very hot days, mainly because of their large size, which gives them a relatively small body area for their size. Sauropod dinosaurs probably had the same problem for the same reasons.

African elephants use their huge ears to get rid of extra heat. The large surface area of their ears allows a lot of heat to escape, just as a wide shallow bowl allows soup to cool quickly.

How do you think sauropods cooled off? Their long slender necks and tails had relatively large surface areas compared to their volumes. Heat probably escaped from their necks and tails. (Some palaeontologists think that the plates of *Stegosaurus* were used to get rid of heat, too.)

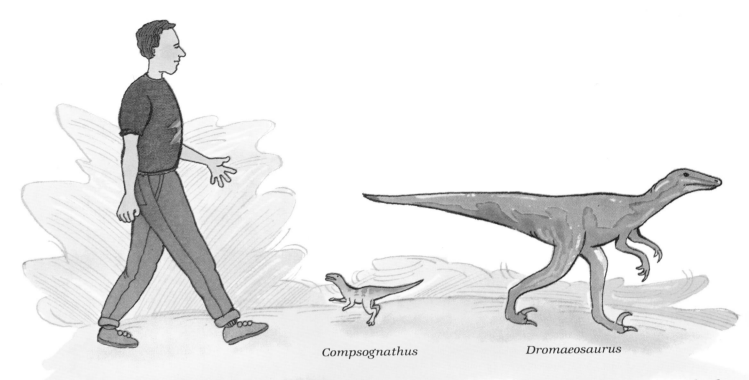

Compsognathus   *Dromaeosaurus*

So much for the large dinosaurs. What about the small ones, such as *Compsognathus* and *Dromaeosaurus*? Like most modern reptiles, they were probably too small to have been able to keep a constant body temperature. But no one knows for certain. Some palaeontologists think that some of the small dinosaurs may have produced as much body heat as modern birds and mammals—that is, they think they had a high metabolism and were therefore warm-blooded.

What about the babies of the large dinosaurs? How big were they? Were they big enough to keep warm during the night? The first dinosaur babies to be found were those of the horned dinosaur *Protoceratops*. They were discovered in 1922 during an expedition to Mongolia by the American Museum of Natural History. *Protoceratops* was a fairly small dinosaur, only about 2 m ($6\frac{1}{2}$ feet) long. Its eggs were about 20 cm

(8 inches) long—hot-dog sized—and hatched into babies that were slightly longer. In addition to the hatchlings, juveniles (young dinosaurs) of varying sizes have been found in nests. What does this tell us? It tells us that the youngsters probably stayed in the nest for some time. They were probably looked after by their parents too, just as birds are today.

Until recently, baby dinosaur bones were rare. Then, in 1978, a remarkable discovery was made in the American southwest. Palaeontologist Jack Horner and his friend Robert Makela, a school teacher, were out searching for baby dinosaur bones in Montana. They had no luck at first and decided to move on to another place. On their way there, they heard about a rock and fossil shop that had some dinosaur bones. They paid a visit to the shop. To their complete surprise, the dinosaur bones

turned out to belong to baby hadrosaurs—just what they had been looking for! When they explained this to the shop owner and told her of their scientific importance, she generously handed over the babies. She then led the two men to the place where she had found the baby bones. Dr. Horner and his friend set to work. Within a short while, they found more babies' bones in the remains of a nest. The nest was 1 metre (3 feet) across. More nests with babies were found on later trips, together with eggs, juveniles and adults. The remains all belonged to a hadrosaur named *Maiasaura*. The babies were about 45 cm (18 inches) long in one of the nests, but about 1 m (3 feet) long in another. Once again, it seems that the youngsters stayed in the nest for a long time and that they were probably looked after by their parents.

Were the hatchling dinosaurs large enough to stay warm at night? Although young dinosaurs were much larger than newly hatched birds, they were probably too small to have kept their body heat at night. Perhaps, instead, they snuggled up close to their parents for warmth. Just imagine a baby dinosaur the size of a cat nestling down against a mother as big as a school bus!

6. The phantom in the stone

Some time during the late 1700s, an unusual fossil
was discovered in a limestone quarry in Germany.
It was a small animal—it would easily fit onto this
page—with unusually thin and delicate bones.
The long, pointed skull was armed with needle-
sharp teeth, but its most remarkable feature was
its hand. The thumb, index and middle fingers
ended in sharp claws that were of normal length,
but the fourth finger was about twice the length
of the body! What sort of an animal was it?

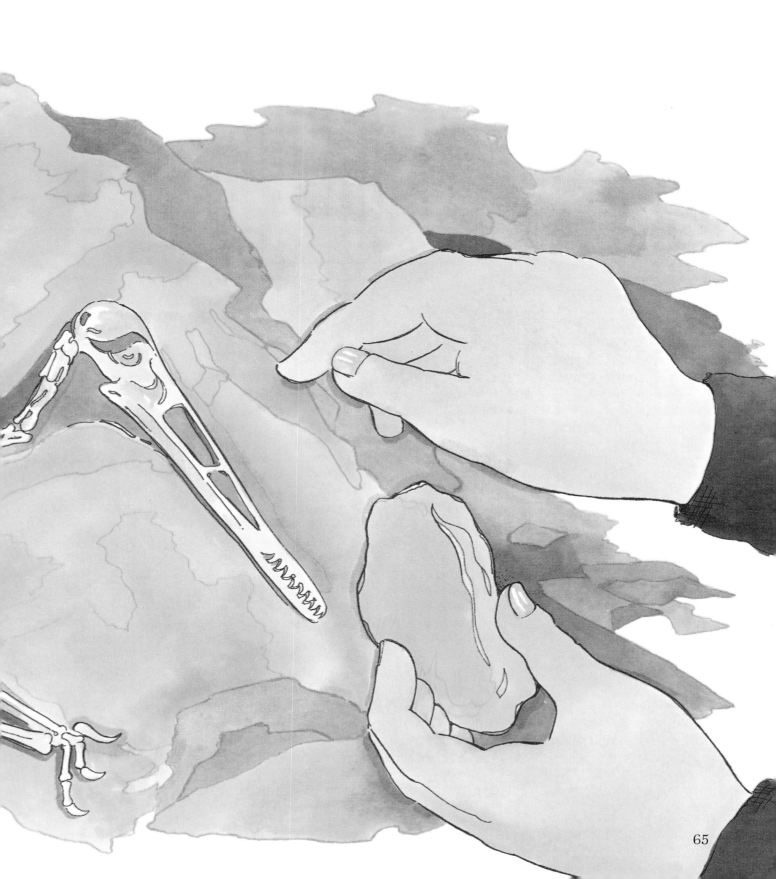

A CLUE IN THE FINGER

The first naturalist to study the fossil could not decide what it was. But Georges Cuvier, the great French anatomist, deduced that the long finger must have been part of a wing that was made of thin skin, like a bat's wing. The new fossil was a flying reptile! This piece of detective work was confirmed some years later when specimens were found with impressions of the thin skin of the wings preserved in the rock. These reptiles were named pterosaurs, meaning "winged reptiles."

Pterosaurs were closely related to dinosaurs and lived at about the same time. Their bony remains have been found all over the world, mostly in rocks that were formed in the sea. This shows that most pterosaurs probably lived close to the sea, like present-day sea birds. And like sea birds, most pterosaurs probably fed on sea foods, such as fish and squids and shrimps.

Unlike birds, pterosaurs did not have feathers, but they may have been furry. Two fossils that have been found show the impressions of what appears to be fur.

Birds have stiff wings. This is because their feathers are stiff and are firmly attached to the wing bones, which run from the elbow to the tip of the finger. Pterosaur wings, in contrast, were very flimsy. The wing was made of thin skin that was supported by only a single finger. This finger, which was very long, formed the leading edge of the wing. Bats have a similar sort of wing, but the skin is stretched between several fingers and it is also attached to the leg.

Pterosaurs range from the starling-sized *Pterodactylus* to the gigantic *Quetzalcoatlus* —the size of a small jet. This is the largest of all flying animals. How did giants such as *Quetzalcoatlus*, with a wing span of 15 m (50 feet), and *Pteranodon*, with a wing span of 7 m (23 feet), ever get off the ground?

Pterosaurs had thin, hollow bones, and lightweight wings. Palaeontologists think they were probably the lightest of all flyers. Their lightweight construction enabled them to get into the air and stay there with the minimum amount of effort. They could probably fly very slowly, too, slower than birds of similar size, and this would have given them a great deal of maneuverability.

Rhamphorhynchus (top left) is a long-tailed pterosaur, while *Pteranodon* (top right) and *Pterodactylus* (left) have short tails.

They were probably the most efficient and graceful gliders that have ever existed.

Over the years, several people have tried to build models of pterosaurs that would fly. Some experiments were more successful than others, but the best of them all was a half-sized model of *Quetzalcoatlus*. This high-tech model was not only lightweight; it had a built-in computer to feed information to a number of electric motors that controlled the movements of the different parts of the body. This allowed the model to make small adjustments in its body throughout the flight, letting it correct for such things as changes in wind movement. As a result it flew superbly, and its body movements were so smooth and natural that it looked as if it were a living pterosaur.

ACTIVITY
A flying lesson

All flyers, from pterosaurs to jumbo jets, rely on their wings to get them into the air and keep them there. Wings produce lift. How? The clue lies in their shape. The top surface is rounded (convex) while the bottom surface is flat or hollowed (concave). When air flows over curved surfaces like this, a lifting force is produced.

Follow these instructions carefully to make a wing that will fly.

You'll need:
o *a pencil and ruler*
o *a sheet of paper 21 × 28 cm (8½ × 11 inches)*
o *scissors*
o *tape*
o *thread*
o *2 garbage-bag ties, 15 cm (6 inches) long, still joined together in a strip*

1. Starting from the top, measure down each side of the sheet and make pencil marks at .5 cm ($\frac{3}{16}$ inch), 5 cm (2 inches) and 10 cm (4 inches). Be precise in your measurements. Draw three lines across the page by joining these pairs of marks.

2. Carefully cut across the bottom line. You will now have a strip of paper with one line close to the top and another running across the middle.

3. Using the ruler as a guide, fold along the two pencil lines—they must both fold the same way. Run the edge of your ruler along each fold, just once, to make them good and sharp.

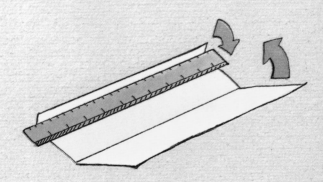

4. Tuck the edge of the longer side into the flap. The longer side will form a gentle curve; the shorter side will be flat. These are the upper and lower surfaces of your wing.

5. Carefully tape the flap to the upper surface of the wing. This will be the back or trailing edge of the wing. The opposite edge is called the leading edge.

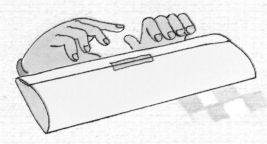

6. To fly your wing, lay it on a table about 15 cm (6 inches) from the table edge. With your chin against the edge of the table, blow a short puff of air. Does your wing take off? If not, try again.

7. To keep your wing from blowing away, tape a piece of thread, 15 cm (6 inches) long, just inside the wing so that the thread is against the leading edge. Repeat at the wing's other end.

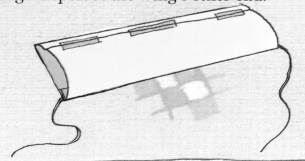

8. Take the two garbage-bag ties, taking care to keep them flat and attached to one another. Lay the wing on top of the ties to form a cross. Tape the wing to the ties at the leading and trailing edges.

9. Lay your aircraft flat on the table, about 15 cm (6 inches) from the edge. Angle the two threads out at the sides, as shown, and tape their free ends to the table.

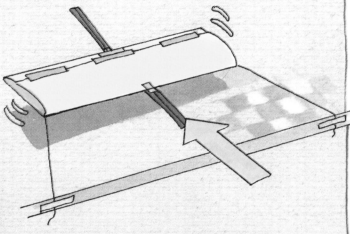

10. With your chin against the edge of the table, gently blow air over the wing. Your wing should take off. If it doesn't, be patient and keep trying. Try changing the strength and perhaps also the angle of your blowing. Try bending the back ends of the garbage-bag ties up slightly. Try using a hair dryer. Hold the dryer at least 15 cm (6 inches) from the edge of the table. Start off with the nozzle below the level of the table and keep it pointed down very slightly. Slowly raise the dryer and your wing should take off. If it starts shaking, remove the dryer and start again. With practice, you'll find that your wing flies quite well.

ACTIVITY

Make a pterosaur glider

This lightweight flying model of a pterosaur is made from things you can find
in your kitchen. It's a bit fiddly to make,
but fun.

You'll need:
- *tape*
- *6 drinking straws*
- *plastic wrap (the stretchy kind you wrap leftovers in)*
- *scissors*
- *clear glue or nail polish*
- *a needle and thread*
- *Plasticine*

1. Tape two straws together side by side
with two pieces of tape, one at the top, the
other at the bottom. Do not tape in the
middle. These straws will be the body of
the pterosaur.

2. Lay a piece of plastic wrap about
40 × 20 cm (16 × 8 inches) on a table.
Tape the corners to the table top, gently
stretching it before you tape.

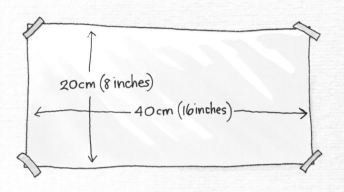

20cm (8 inches)
40cm (16 inches)

3. Place the two taped straws in the
middle of the plastic wrap parallel to the
short sides. Place a third straw on one side
of the pterosaur's body straws, about 4 cm
($1\frac{1}{2}$ inches) from one end. This will become
one of the wings. This wing straw has to
be at right angles to the body straws and
just touching them. Do the same thing
with a fourth straw on the other side.

4cm
($1\frac{1}{2}$ inches)

4. Pick up one of the wing straws, run glue along its length, and put it back again, glue-side down. Repeat with the other straw. Remove the two body straws.

5. When the glue has dried, run glue along the top surface of each of the two wing straws. Before the glue has a chance to dry, fold the top flap of plastic wrap over the top of the wing straws and press down. This will glue the wrap firmly to the wing straws. When the glue has dried, trim off the remains of the top flap of plastic wrap.

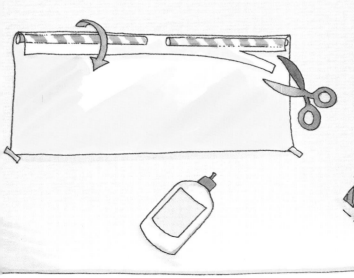

6. Put the body straws back in place with their front ends extending 4 cm ($1\frac{1}{2}$ inches) beyond the wing straws. Make sure they fit snugly between the wing straws. (If there isn't enough room, trim the wing straws until the body fits.) Tape the ends of the wing straws to the body straws. Trim the plastic wrap so that it's only 13 cm (5 inches) wide.

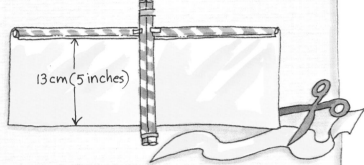

13 cm (5 inches)

7. Hold the free bottom edge of the plastic wrap in the middle and pinch it up into a fold. Now tuck this fold of wrap into the gap between the two body straws and pull it through from the other side. This will pull the wing tips back as shown. Crumple the fold of plastic wrap up to keep it where it is. The two wing tips should be pulled back by the same amount (otherwise your pterosaur will be lopsided). This can be adjusted by pulling more plastic wrap through the gap on one side or the other.

8. Thread the needle with a single strand of thread about 50 cm (20 inches) long. Push the needle through the wing tip of one of the wing straws. Pull the thread all the way through and tie off the end. Run the thread to the top end of the body and pull on it until it is taut. Hold it in place with a small piece of tape. Take the thread across to the other wing tip and push the needle through the tip of the straw as before. Pull the thread through and pull on it until it is taut, as on the other side. Cut off the excess thread, leaving a loose end about 2.5 cm (1 inch) long. Attach this loose end to the straw at the wing tip with a small piece of tape.

9. At this stage, the wings should have the same amount of backward sweep and should be held in position by the pulling of the thread. If the wings are not even, you can fix this by pulling on the wing fold that is tucked between the gap between the body straws. You can also help by tightening or loosening the wing threads. When you are happy with the setting of the wings, tape down the wing fold with a few pieces of tape.

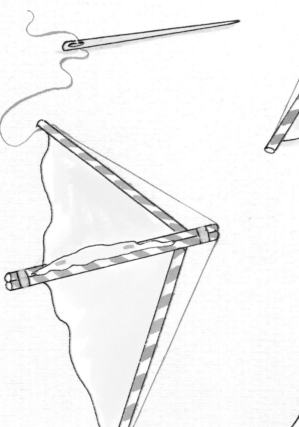

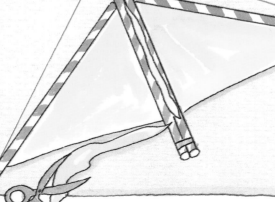

10. Trim the trailing edges of the wings by cutting with the scissors along a straight line from the wing tip to the body.

11. Tape the two remaining straws together. They will become the top part of the body. Position these taped straws over the other two body straws so that the plastic wrap is sandwiched between them. Tape the two pairs of straws firmly together at both ends to complete the body.

12. Tape the wing straws to the sides of the new body section. The wings should be quite stiff now. If they are not, it is probably because they are not firmly taped to the sides of the body.

13. Add a small piece of Plasticine to the nose, and another to the tail.

14. You're now ready to test-fly your pterosaur glider. It will probably not fly properly at first because it is not correctly balanced. It should glide with its nose down. If it doesn't, add a little more Plasticine to the nose. If it is nose-heavy, remove some Plasticine.

Your glider is like a real pterosaur:
- it is lightly built
- the wing surface is a thin skin
- the wing is supported only at its leading edge

Each wing of your glider is saved from collapsing by the tension (pull) in the thread. In pterosaurs, this function was probably carried out by a muscle. Clues that this muscle existed have been found in some pterosaur skeletons.

7. Sea monsters

The pebbles crunched beneath her boots as she hurried along the beach on the south coast of England. A chill wind blew off the sea, a wind so cold that it seemed to pass right through her. Her cloak was an old one of her brother's, and it was far too big for her. Poor Mary, poor brother Joseph and poor Mamma. Poor Papa too—oh, how she missed him. Never again would they go along the beach here in Lyme Regis in search of fossils.

She hunted for fossils alone now, and not just for the love of it, either. Since her father's death, the money she got from selling fossils to the summer visitors kept her family from the poor-house. She'd get a good price for her latest find. Well, to be absolutely fair, it was her brother who actually discovered it. But Joseph wasn't very interested in fossils any more, now that he was working in the furniture business.

She moved up the beach to the foot of the cliffs and peered intently at one of the limestone ledges. To an untrained eye, this slab of grey rock—almost as thick as her arm was long—looked like all the others.

The ichthyosaur that Mary Anning found can still be seen at the Natural History Museum in London, England.

But it was not like them—it contained a most unusual fossil. Her experienced eye could see the pointed teeth and the crocodile shape of its skull. She reached out and touched it. A small hand, a small twelve-year-old's hand. She couldn't even begin to guess what sort of an animal it was, nor how long it had been there, waiting to be discovered. Time had no meaning for Mary Anning at that moment. She forgot about the cold. She forgot about the problems that troubled her young life. Here she was with a sea monster, the likes of which had never been seen before, and nothing else mattered.

With a sudden start she came back to the present, to the year 1812. She couldn't stand there day-dreaming— there was work to be done, money to be earned, a family to support. She reached into her basket, pulled out a hammer and chisel and set to work.

75

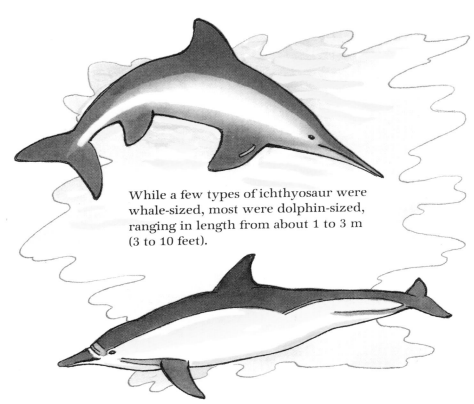

While a few types of ichthyosaur were whale-sized, most were dolphin-sized, ranging in length from about 1 to 3 m (3 to 10 feet).

Mary Anning had discovered a complete skull, some vertebrae and part of the shoulder of a reptile that lived in the sea at the same time as dinosaurs lived on land. These marine reptiles were later named ichthyosaurs, meaning "fish-lizards."

The first scientist who examined Mary's specimen —a man named Sir Everard Home—was confused by the clues. All ichthyosaurs had fins instead of legs, most of them had a tail like that of a fish and most were streamlined. Home couldn't make up his mind whether the metre- (yard-) long skull belonged to a fish or some new species of crocodile. But some of the other scientists of the day correctly identified the specimen as being a reptile that looked like a fish.

Sir Richard Owen, one of the greatest palaeontologists of the last century, corrected Home's mistakes, then made one of his own. His blooper had to do with the tails of ichthyosaurs.

By the time Owen became interested in ichthyosaurs, several skeletons had been found. Some of these showed odd-looking bends in the backbone, in the tail region. Owen was very interested in these tail bends and thought they had happened after the animals had died. He believed that when ichthyosaurs were alive, their tails were straight.

Owen was an important man, so his ideas were accepted and drawings showed ichthyosaurs with straight tails. They were also shown as being able to haul themselves up on land like seals. And life-sized models of ichthyosaurs built under Owen's supervision had—you guessed it— straight tails.

Not long after Owen died, some ichthyosaurs were found in Germany. They were so well preserved that the entire outline of the body was visible in addition to the skeleton. Owen had been wrong. The tail *was* bent. Ichthyosaurs had a tail fin like that of a fish. The German fossils also showed that ichthyosaurs had a fin on the top of their backs, too, just like a fish. Because ichthyosaurs had fish-like

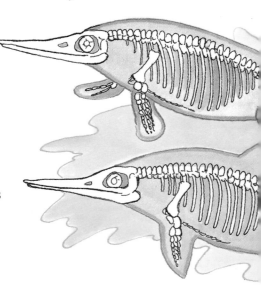

bodies and tails, they would not have been able to haul themselves up on land.

Not all ichthyosaurs had tail bends. Even those that did are sometimes found with straight tails because of the way their bodies have been preserved. This can be very confusing for poor palaeontologists! Fortunately there's a way of telling whether an ichthyosaur had a tail bend or not. The clue is in the backbone.

The round discs of bone (vertebrae) that make up the vertebral column (backbone) are the same thickness all the way around — top, bottom and sides — except at the tail bend. Here the vertebrae are much thicker at the top than at the bottom. These wedge-shaped vertebrae give the tail its bend. Try "Tails bones tell" and see for yourself.

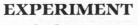

EXPERIMENT
Tails bones tell

Slice a banana into some vertebrae (backbones) and see what you discover about tail bends of ichthyosaurs.

You'll need:
○ *a banana*
○ *a blunt table knife*
○ *a ruler*

1. Peel the banana and slice off eight discs, 1 cm ($\frac{1}{2}$ inch) thick. Slice off four wedge-shaped pieces — about 1 cm ($\frac{1}{2}$ inch) thick at the top and 0.5 cm ($\frac{1}{4}$ inch) thick at the bottom.

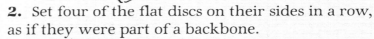

2. Set four of the flat discs on their sides in a row, as if they were part of a backbone.
3. Add the four wedge-shaped discs, making sure that their thickest parts are all at the top.

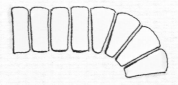

4. Add the rest of the ordinary discs.

The wedge-shaped discs cause the banana "tail" to bend. When palaeontologists see wedge-shaped bones, they know that the ichthyosaur they came from had a tail bend, too. If the bones are encased in rock, an X-ray can be taken (for more on X-rays and fossil bones, see page 19).

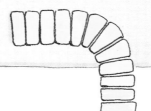

SHAPE AND SPEED

Ichthyosaurs had stream-lined bodies—a clue that they lived in water and that they were fast swimmers. The front of the body was pointed, the thickest part of the body lay about a third of the way back and the rest of the body was gently tapered. We see this shape in certain animals, such as fish, dolphins and birds, and people have used it in vehicles, such as yachts, submarines, airplanes and even in cars. What's so special about the stream-lined shape? The answer is a bit of a drag.

When an object moves through air or water, it meets with resistance. This resistance, which slows it down, is called "drag."

EXPERIMENT
A real drag

Want to experience drag? You do every time you run or swim. The air or water hits against your body, slowing you down.

You'll need:
○ *a piece of cardboard, at least as large as this book*

EXPERIMENT
A tow in the tub

Make two Plasticine mod-els—one streamlined and the other not—then test them out for drag in the bathtub.

You'll need:
○ *Plasticine*
○ *a blunt table knife*
○ *2 paper clips*
○ *4 drinking straws*
○ *scissors*
○ *a needle and thread*

1. Roll the Plasticine into a log 15 cm (6 inches) long and 2 cm ($\frac{3}{4}$ inch) wide.

2. Using the knife, cut the log in half, then trim one of the pieces as shown. Smooth its edges to make a streamlined shape.

3. Break off the inner loop of each paper clip by bend-ing it backward and for-ward. Push the loop into the front end of each Plasti-cine model so that only a small part of the loop sticks out. This is the tow-ing loop.

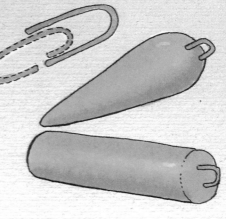

4. You now have two models, one streamlined and the other rod-shaped. Can you think of any other difference between them besides shape? Of course, the rod-shaped one is much heavier. This can affect the results of your experiment, so you've got to trim some weight off it.

78

1. Hold the cardboard vertically and quickly move it through the air so that the air pushes against its flat surface. Feel the drag force.

2. Repeat, but hold the cardboard horizontally so it slices through the air. The air is now pushing against the edge rather than the flat surface. Notice how the drag force is much smaller?

Being very thin reduces drag, but that's not practical. The best way is to be streamlined.

5. Using one of the straws as a corer, hollow out the rod-shaped model, as shown. The straw soon gets blocked up with Plasticine, so you have to keep cutting it off with scissors. Keep on coring until the two models feel about the same weight.

6. Using the needle, attach a piece of the thread to the end of each of the remaining two straws and tie it securely. Tie the other end of the thread to the towing loop of your model. Make the tow thread about 3 cm (1 inch) long. You now have a handle and a towing line for each model.

7. Try pulling each of the models through the water —use the whole length of the tub and see how fast you can go.

Was the streamlined model easier to pull? That shows it had the smaller drag. The ichthyosaur's streamlined shape let it swim fast with the least amount of drag. But what was the purpose of its fins? Find out by trying "Finny fins."

79

Your model lacks stability, but you can fix that with some fins.

EXPERIMENT
Finny fins

Why do fishes and ichthyosaurs have fins? Try this experiment to find out.

You'll need:

o *a streamlined Plasticine model (to make one, follow Steps 1, 2, 3 and 6 of "A tow in the tub")*
o *scissors*
o *a small aluminum baking tray (you will be cutting this into pieces, so ask permission before using)*
o *a blunt table knife*

1. Put your model in the tub, 8 to 10 cm (3 to 4 inches) below the surface, and tow it up and down. Try wiggling the towing handle, and try making some turns.

You'll probably find that your model moves quite well in the water but that it wiggles and jiggles a bit.

2. Cut three triangles from the aluminum baking trays. One of the triangles, which will be the back fin (called the dorsal fin), should have two sides about 2 cm ($\frac{3}{4}$ inch) long. (The third side will be longer.) The other two triangles, which will become the hind fins, should be smaller. Make two of their sides each 1.5 cm ($\frac{5}{16}$ inch) long.

3. Use the knife to cut a slit the same length as your dorsal fin in the middle of the back of your Plasticine model. Push the aluminum dorsal fin into this slit as shown. Smooth the Plasticine all around it. Your model should begin to look a bit like something from the movie *Jaws*.

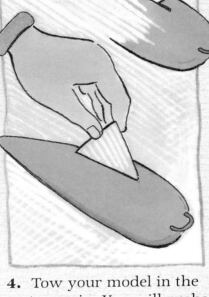

4. Tow your model in the water again. You will probably find that it doesn't wiggle so much—the dorsal fin has improved its stability—but you can still do better.

5. Make a slit low down on the left side of your model, behind the dorsal fin. Put one of the remaining aluminum fins into this slit. Repeat for the right side.

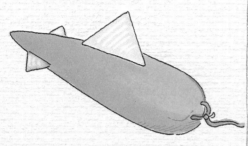

6. Adjust the hind fins so that they tilt downward by the same amount. When you view your model from the back, the three fins should look like the flight feathers of a dart.

7. Return your model to the water. This time you should find it is much more stable—it no longer wiggles and jiggles when towed.

Experiments like this show us that the most likely purpose of the dorsal fin and the paired hind fins of ichthyosaurs was for greater stability when swimming.

What's the most important clue to an animal's diet? If you said its teeth, you've earned your dinosaur detective's badge. Most ichthyosaurs had lots of slender, sharply pointed teeth and when their jaws closed, the upper and lower teeth meshed together like a trap. Many modern animals, such as dolphins, seals and gavials (long-snouted crocodiles), have teeth like this.

What do you think animals with lots of sharp, slender teeth would have eaten? Something slippery and difficult to catch? If you said fish, congratulations. These sorts of teeth are also very good for catching squids, slippery animals with long tentacles that are related to the octopus.

During the days of the ichthyosaurs, the seas teemed with belemnites,

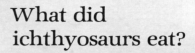

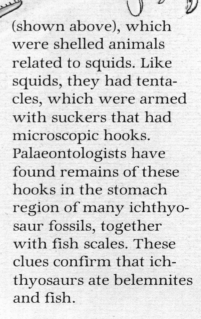

(shown above), which were shelled animals related to squids. Like squids, they had tentacles, which were armed with suckers that had microscopic hooks. Palaeontologists have found remains of these hooks in the stomach region of many ichthyosaur fossils, together with fish scales. These clues confirm that ichthyosaurs ate belemnites and fish.

Baby ichthyosaurs

The year was 1845 and Chaning Pearce, an English fossil collector, was busy in his study. He was chipping away at the rock that covered an ichthyosaur skeleton. When he got to the pelvic region, he was surprised to find a tiny ichthyosaur skull. Further chipping revealed the rest of the skeleton. Was it an unfortunate victim of cannibalism? No—it was an unborn baby ichthyosaur. Since then, more ichthyosaurs with embryos (unborn young) have been found. That means that, unlike the dinosaurs, ichthyosaurs didn't lay eggs. They gave birth to live young.

Long-necked plesiosaur

Mosasaur

OTHER SEA REPTILES

A few years after discovering her first ichthyosaur, Mary Anning discovered a second group of marine reptiles that were new to science. These reptiles were named plesiosaurs, meaning "near lizards." Some plesiosaurs had large heads and short necks and tails. Others had small heads with long necks and tails—one palaeontologist said they looked like a snake strung through the body of a turtle.

Plesiosaurs came in a wide range of sizes. *Kronosaurus*, discovered in Australia, was one of the largest. Its head alone was 2.4 m (8 feet) long. It may have preyed upon other marine reptiles. Most plesiosaurs were much smaller than *Kronosaurus*. Like their cousins the ichthyosaurs, many were the size of a dolphin and probably fed on fish.

The third major group of marine reptiles, the mosasaurs, were large lizards, averaging about 6 to 9 m (20 to 30 feet) long. As you already know, some of them attacked ammonites (see page 18). They probably also fed on fish and perhaps other marine reptiles, too. Mosasaurs did not appear until towards the end of the Cretaceous Period, by which time the ichthyosaurs had already become extinct.

Ichthyosaurs, plesiosaurs and mosasaurs were all reptiles and breathed through lungs, rather than gills as fish do. We know that ichthyosaurs carried their young inside their bodies and gave birth at sea, like modern whales. Although there is no clear evidence about plesiosaurs and mosasaurs, it seems likely that they did, too. Like the dinosaurs, they all became extinct at the end of the Cretaceous.

Kronosaurus
Short-necked plesiosaur

8. The end of the dinosaurs

Dinosaurs disappeared from Earth at the end of the Cretaceous Period, about 65 million years ago. To a palaeontologist, their disappearance was sudden. To see how sudden, let's take a trip to Hell Creek, Montana, to hunt for the last of the dinosaurs.

It's hot and dry and the sun beats down without mercy. You want to stop for a drink but you've just had one. No wonder they call these dry places the badlands. As you crunch over the crumbling earth, your boots are in the Cretaceous Period and your head is in the Tertiary Period. You can find dinosaur bones down by your feet, but you could search the layers above your head for a thousand years and not find a single one. The rocks you're clambering over took a very long time to build up. It took many thousands of years to form 2.5 cm (1 inch) of rock. So the rock layers your boots are crunching over are several hundred thousand years older than the ones at eye level.

The rocks tell us that dinosaurs died out suddenly—their fossil remains are present in the lower layers but not in the upper ones. But how sudden is sudden? The rocks that contain the last of the dinosaurs are about 65 million years old, give or take about 500 000 years. That's as accurate as our dating can be. So two dinosaurs could be found in the same Cretaceous rocks in different parts of the world and still be as much as 500 000 years apart. Because of this 500 000-year time span, it's impossible to know if the last of the dinosaurs all became extinct at precisely the same time. Their extinction may have been sudden, or it may have been gradual, happening over 500 000 years.

What happened to the dinosaurs and all those other reptiles anyway? Why did they all disappear from the Earth at the end of the Mesozoic Era? Palaeontologists have pondered this question for a hundred years and have come up with many different ideas.

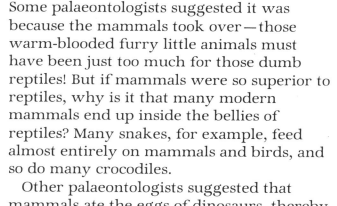

Some palaeontologists suggested it was because the mammals took over—those warm-blooded furry little animals must have been just too much for those dumb reptiles! But if mammals were so superior to reptiles, why is it that many modern mammals end up inside the bellies of reptiles? Many snakes, for example, feed almost entirely on mammals and birds, and so do many crocodiles.

Other palaeontologists suggested that mammals ate the eggs of dinosaurs, thereby wiping them all out. No doubt some mammals did eat dinosaur eggs, but probably just as many young mammals were gobbled up by dinosaurs. Besides, why should the mammals have waited until the end of the Mesozoic to develop a taste for dinosaur eggs? Mammals, after all, had been around for about as long as the dinosaurs.

Another idea was that great plagues of diseases spread through the reptiles, wiping them all out. But what sort of diseases would kill only reptiles? And if there had been such diseases, why didn't they kill off all the reptiles, not just the dinosaurs? These are only a few of the ideas that have been suggested, but none of them fully answers the question.

CLUES FROM OUTER SPACE

In the late 1970s, scientists studying some Italian rocks formed at the very end of the Cretaceous Period were surprised to find unusually high amounts of a metal called iridium. Iridium is very rare on Earth and is usually found in such small amounts that it can be measured only by using special equipment. Although rare on Earth, iridium is often found in meteorites and other extra-terrestrial bodies. This led scientists to wonder whether the iridium in the rock samples from Italy had actually come from outer space.

More samples of late Cretaceous rocks were collected from other parts of the world. The results were the same—the samples all contained unusually high levels of iridium. What was the explanation? The most likely answer seemed to be that the Earth had been struck by a large asteroid (a large stony boulder bigger than a meteorite) at the end of the Cretaceous Period. Based on their estimates of how much iridium was present around the globe, the scientists calculated that the asteroid was big. How big? About 10 km (6 miles) across! What's more, it would have been travelling very fast. Astronomers estimate that asteroids reach speeds of about 90 000 km/h (55 000 mph). If a giant asteroid had struck the Earth at that speed, it would create an explosion bigger than that of all of the bombs in the world put together. The heat generated would have vaporized the aster-oid, leaving a crater in the Earth about 100 km (60 miles) across. A great cloud of iridium-rich dust and smoke would have been thrown high into the atmosphere and spread around the world. Such an event would have caused major environmental changes. For a start, the dust would have

Triceratops

blocked out much of the light from the Sun. Some scientists think there would have been total darkness for as long as a year, but others think the effects would have been less drastic. In any event, many plants would have died because they lacked the sunlight they needed to survive. This in turn would have caused the animals that fed on them to starve. There would also have been a drop in the Earth's temperatures, which would have killed off the less hardy plants and animals.

Although many palaeontologists are con-vinced that the end of the dinosaurs was caused by an asteroid impact, others are equally convinced that it was not. Some scientists have pointed out that the iridium

Thescelosaurus

Edmontosaurus

dinosaurs but not their close relatives, the crocodiles? Why would it kill off all the pterosaurs but leave the birds? And what about the fact that some dinosaurs and other reptiles had already died out before the end of the Cretaceous? The ichthyosaurs, for example, became extinct about 25 million years before the end of the Cretaceous. Some groups of dinosaurs, like the sauropods and stegosaurs, had dwindled away almost to nothing before the end of the Cretaceous.

So what does a dinosaur detective make of all these conflicting clues? It's like trying to solve a whole series of murders that happened 65 million years ago. This mystery would probably be too difficult even for Sherlock Holmes. Is there a solution?

Probably an asteroid did strike the Earth at the end of the Cretaceous. But this was already a time of great environmental upheaval. There was a considerable amount of volcanic activity, mountain ranges were being formed and inland seas were drying up. These changes had a big effect on the climate. It became cooler, with a much greater difference between summer and winter temperatures. Such climatic changes probably had more effect on the dinosaurs than on the mammals and birds. This was partly because of their large size, their low metabolic rates (compared with birds and mammals) and their absence of fur or other body covering. Imagine a 20-tonne (ton) dinosaur trying to huddle in a crevice on a cold winter's night to keep warm.

Many groups of Mesozoic reptiles had either become extinct before the impact, or were already on the way out at that time. The asteroid impact may have been just one more thing going wrong for the dinosaurs. The days of the dinosaurs were numbered and, asteroid or not, they probably would not have survived until today.

may not have come from an asteroid at all but from volcanoes instead. Iridium is certainly found in the ash from erupting volcanoes, and geologists know that the end of the Cretaceous was a time of much volcanic activity.

There are other problems with the "big bang" extinction idea. Why would the effects of an asteroid impact wipe out some of the reptiles but not the mammals and birds? Why would it destroy all the

BACK TO THE FUTURE

Imagine you're an interplanetary palaeontologist of the future—digging up fossils on the earth thousands of years from now. The rocks in which you're digging were formed during the 1990s—during the Civilization Period. Just think what you might find in the rocks. You would see the end of mammoths, mastodons, sabre-tooth cats, cave bears, giant ground sloths and all the other animals that became extinct at the end of the last Ice Age. A few centimetres (inches) of rock represent many thousands of years, so all the extinctions seem to have taken place at about the same time. Some palaeontologists blame these extinctions on the changes in climate, but others think it might have been caused by over-hunting.

Higher up in the layers of rock, you would see the disappearance of hundreds of species of birds, frogs, toads, lizards, snakes, fish, land mammals, whales, dolphins. . . . Add to this list countless species of insects and other animals without backbones and numerous species of plants. The extinction event at the end of the Civilization Period was obviously much bigger than the one at the end of the Cretaceous. What went wrong?

You've just spotted a small piece of bone sticking out of the rock. Will it turn out to be a whole skeleton? The chances are slim, but you take out your hammer and chisels and set to work. By the end of the day, you've uncovered several bones and you're pretty sure there are lots more still buried in the rock. You've got a hunch that you've found the whole skeleton.

While you've been digging, you've also been collecting rock samples for analysis back at the lab. So far iridium has never been found in these sorts of rocks—unlike the rocks at the end of the Cretaceous.

Therefore it doesn't look as if the extinctions at the end of the Civilization Period had anything to do with an asteroid impact. But plenty of other unusual things have been found—things such as soot, lead, mercury, plutonium and other radioactive elements and all sorts of chemicals. You begin to wonder whether the extinctions were caused by all of these harmful pollutants in the environment. But there's something wrong with this idea. If pollution had been to blame, why didn't it kill off all the species? It's true that hundreds of species became extinct, but many others survived. In fact, one particular species—the one you've been digging up—seems to have thrived. They were the dominant land animals, and you suspect that it was they who were responsible for the downfall of all the other species.

After nearly a week of chiselling away at the rock, you have collected an almost complete skeleton. You've carefully packed it into a crate ready to send back to your museum. All you have to do now is write the label. You take a thick felt pen from your pocket and write on the crate in large black letters, first the Latin name, then the common name:

89

9. Are dinosaurs really extinct?

Some scientists think that dinosaurs are still alive today. No, they don't think there are sauropods crashing around in some remote jungle, or some hadrosaurs munching their way through a tropical grassland. The dinosaurs they are thinking about are the ones the rest of us call birds. This may sound crazy to you, but it's just the way that these scientists group animals together. They think that birds should be called dinosaurs because the two groups are so closely related. Most other scientists think that dinosaurs should be classified separately from birds. Regardless of this disagreement among the experts, most palaeontologists agree that birds actually evolved from dinosaurs.

You may find it hard to believe that a sparrow is even remotely related to

Tyrannosaurus, but there is a lot of evidence to support the case. Reptiles and birds both lay the same sorts of eggs, some of their internal parts are similar, and they both have a scaly skin (in birds this shows clearly only on the legs and feet).

The idea that birds evolved from dinosaurs is not new. It actually dates back to the last century and the discovery of an important fossil named *Archaeopteryx*. This pigeon-sized fossil has a combination of bird-like and reptilian features. For example, it has feathers and wings like a bird, but each wing has three clawed fingers like a dinosaur. And it had a long bony tail like a dinosaur's.

If you look at the skeleton of a modern bird it doesn't look very much like a dinosaur. This is mainly because the bones of a bird's skeleton join together as it grows, hiding its similarities with dinosaurs. However, if you compared the skeleton of a bird *embryo* (an unhatched, developing bird in which the individual bones are still separate) with that of a dinosaur, you would see many similarities.

ACTIVITY

Dissect a dinosaur descendant

Since bird embryos aren't readily available, let's take a look at the next best thing—a chicken from your favourite take-out. To make sure that you get the most tender, mouth-watering meal, chicken restaurants usually serve only very young birds. Their bones have not completely joined together, so you can still see some dinosaurian features that are not visible in older birds. You will also be able to see a few other dinosaurian features that birds never lose.

You'll need:

○ *a whole cooked chicken*
○ *a pot with lid*
○ *somebody to share the chicken with you*

1. Enjoy your meal, but be sure to save all the bones.
2. With the help of an adult, put all the bones from the chicken into the pot, cover them with water and bring the water to the boil. Turn down the heat to its lowest setting, cover the pan with a lid, and let the contents simmer for about an hour.
3. Ask your adult helper to remove the pot from the stove. Run cold water over the bones until they're cold, then drain off the water. Remove the remains of the meat and skin with your fingers. (If the bones do not come clean easily, pop them back in the pot and continue simmering for another half hour or so.) When the bones are clean, spread them out on a plate and let them dry overnight before proceeding.
4. With the help of the picture here, find the following bones: femur (thigh bone), tibia (shin bone), humerus (upper arm bone). Notice how similar these are to the same bones in dinosaurs.

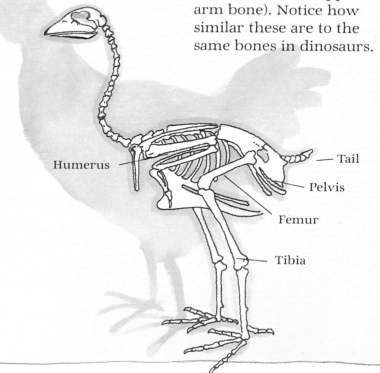

Humerus — Tail — Pelvis — Femur — Tibia

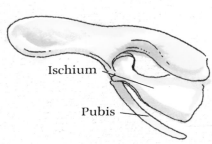

Ischium

Pubis

5. Find the pelvis. If your bird is young enough, you'll be able to see that the pelvis has three prongs, like that of a dinosaur. One of the obvious differences is that the two lower prongs, the pubis and ischium, swing back in birds. (A bird embryo would look even more like a dinosaur.)

Vertebrae

6. Find the tail. Notice that there are at least six bones (vertebrae). This is a very short tail compared with a dinosaur's, but it does show that birds have the remnants of a bony tail.

7. Find the wing. By comparing this with the picture, find the thumb. This is the only free finger in a bird's hand. If you looked at the hand of an embryo, you'd find it still had three free fingers. The bird's thumb, called the *allula*, is often used when birds land. You can see a pigeon's thumb at the leading edge of its wing, where the wing bends. Watch a pigeon land and, if you are lucky, you'll see a small object pop out that looks like a miniature wing. This is the pigeon's thumb. This thumb is an evolutionary link with the pigeon's ancestors—those magnificent dinosaurs that roamed the earth more than 65 million years ago.

Allula

Activities and experiments

Index

Glossary

Binocular vision: the ability to see an object with both eyes at the same time. This helps animals judge distances and is especially useful to hunters.

Biped: an animal that walks on two legs

Carnivore: an animal that eats meat

CAT-scan: an X-ray that shows pictures of imaginary slices through people or even dinosaur skeletons

Centre of mass: the balance point of a body. Sometimes called the centre of gravity.

Cold-blooded: an animal, such as a snake or lizard, that depends on the sun to keep its body warm

Cretaceous Period: the last period of the Mesozoic Era (Age of Reptiles). It lasted from 145 to 65 million years ago.

Drag: the resistance that slows objects down as they move through air or water

Erosion: the wearing away of rocks and fossils by water, sun, ice, wind, rain, etc.

Fossil: the preserved remains of a plant or animal that died long ago

Herbivore: an animal that eats plants

Ichthyosaur: a swimming reptile, with a fish-like body, that lived at the same time as dinosaurs

Inertia: the tendency of things to stay where they are

Jurassic Period: the middle period of the Mesozoic Era (Age of Reptiles). It lasted from 208 to 145 million years ago.

Mesozoic Era: sometimes called the Age of Reptiles because this is when the dinosaurs roamed the Earth

Metabolism: the chemical reactions that take place in the cells of living things. These reactions produce heat.

Palaeontologist: a scientist who studies fossils

Pelvis: the part of the skeleton to which the hind legs are attached. Sometimes called the hips.

Plesiosaur: a swimming reptile that lived at the same time as dinosaurs. Some had long necks and small heads, while others had short necks and long heads.

Predator: an animal that hunts other animals for food

Prey: an animal that is hunted by other animals as food

Pterosaur: a flying reptile that lived at the same time as the dinosaurs

Quadruped: an animal that walks on four legs

Scavenger: an animal that feeds on the dead bodies of other animals

Sediment: particles, such as sand and mud, that may eventually become joined together to form sedimentary rock

Specimen: object of interest to scientists. For example, some palaeontologists study dinosaur specimens.

Trackway: a series of footprints

Triassic Period: the first period of the Mesozoic Era (Age of Reptiles). It lasted from 245 to 208 million years ago.

Vertebrate: an animal that has a vertebral column (backbone)

Warm-blooded: an animal, such as a bird or mammal, that keeps its body warm through its metabolism (see above)

Answers

Would you make a good dinosaur detective?, page 9

If you scored more than 6 points, you have the makings of a dynamite dinosaur detective.
If you scored 3 to 6 points, you'd solve some mysteries, but not others.
If you scored fewer than 3 points, you'd better work on your detective skills.

Spot the imposters, page 14

The animals are: 1. pterosaur, 2. edaphosaur, 3. ichthyosaur, 4. mammoth, 5. stegosaur, 6. plesiosaur, 7. hadrosaur, 8. titanothere, 9. dromaeosaur. Animals 1, 2, 3, 4, 6 and 8 are imposters.

Eye clues, page 36

Tyrannosaurus and *Nanotyrannus* were probably both predators. *Edmontosaurus* and *Triceratops* were probably both hunted.

Sherlock Holmes in the snow, page 49

Track A belongs to the jogger and track B belongs to the walker. You can tell who was jogging because that track has the longer stride length. The paths cross only once, near the middle of the illustration. If you examine that area, you can see that track A overprints on track B. That means that A jogged in the snow after B walked in it.

You can use these same deductions when playing this game outside in the snow. You can even tell which tracks belong to which friend. Just compare the pattern on the bottom of their boots with the pattern of their footprints. (If one of your friends is much bigger than the other, it might be difficult to tell who was moving faster because stride length also increases with body size.)

Why big things stay warm, page 59

Cutting up a large potato is the same as changing it into a number of smaller potatoes. Smaller potatoes, or pieces of potato, have a greater surface-area-to-volume ratio than large ones. Since objects lose heat from their surfaces, smaller potatoes lose heat more quickly.

Cool ants, page 60

When you first take the cold ants out of the fridge, they move much more slowly than the others. However, they warm up quickly because of their small size. Being so small, ants have a very large surface-area-to-volume ratio. Like any animal or object, they lose and gain heat through their body surface, so their relatively large body surface means they change temperature rapidly.